New Materialism:
Interviews & Cartographies

New Metaphysics

Series Editors: Graham Harman and Bruno Latour

The world is due for a resurgence of original speculative metaphysics. The New Metaphysics series aims to provide a safe house for such thinking amidst the demoralizing caution and prudence of professional academic philosophy. We do not aim to bridge the analytic-continental divide, since we are equally impatient with nail-filing analytic critique and the continental reverence for dusty textual monuments. We favor instead the spirit of the intellectual gambler, and wish to discover and promote authors who meet this description. Like an emergent recording company, what we seek are traces of a new metaphysical 'sound' from any nation of the world. The editors are open to translations of neglected metaphysical classics, and will consider secondary works of especial force and daring. But our main interest is to stimulate the birth of disturbing masterpieces of twenty-first century philosophy.

Rick Dolphijn and Iris van der Tuin

New Materialism:
Interviews & Cartographies

O
OPEN HUMANITIES PRESS

An imprint of MPublishing – University of Michigan Library, Ann Arbor, 2012

First edition published by Open Humanities Press
Freely available online at http://hdl.handle.net/2027/spo.11515701.0001.001

Copyright © 2012 Rick Dolphijn and Iris van der Tuin and the respective authors
This is an open access book, licensed under a Creative Commons By Attribution Share Alike license. Under this license, authors allow anyone to download, reuse, reprint, modify, distribute, and/or copy this book so long as the authors and source are cited and resulting derivative works are licensed under the same or similar license. No permission is required from the authors or the publisher. Statutory fair use and other rights are in no way affected by the above. Read more about the license at creativecommons.org/licenses/by-sa/3.0

Design by Katherine Gillieson
Cover Illustration by Tammy Lu

The cover illustration is copyright Tammy Lu 2012, used under a
Creative Commons By Attribution license (CC-BY).

ISBN-10 1-60785-281-0
ISBN-13 978-1-60785-281-0

Open Humanities Press is an international, scholar-led open access publishing collective whose mission is to make leading works of contemporary critical thought freely available worldwide. Books published under the Open Humanities Press imprint at MPublishing are produced through a unique partnership between OHP's editorial board and the University of Michigan Library, which provides a library-based managing and production support infrastructure to facilitate scholars to publish leading research in book form.

MPublishing
www.publishing.umich.edu

OPEN HUMANITIES PRESS
www.openhumanitiespress.org

Contents

Acknowledgements   9

Introduction: What May I Hope For?   13

I   Interviews

1. Interview with Rosi Braidotti   19
2. Interview with Manuel DeLanda   38
3. Interview with Karen Barad   48
4. Interview with Quentin Meillassoux   71

II   Cartographies

Introduction: A "New Tradition" in Thought   85

5. The Transversality of New Materialism   93
6. Pushing Dualism to an Extreme   115
7. Sexual Differing   137
8. The End of (Wo)Man   158

Bibliography   181

Permissions   195

Matter can receive a form, and within this form-matter relation lies the ontogenesis.

– Gilbert Simondon

Acknowledgements

This book is the result of intense interaction between the two authors and many others. Giving names to the particular elements that form this swarm is an impossible but necessary undertaking, since the two names on the cover of this book definitely do not exhaust what made the book. Most of all, of course, the four wise and generous minds that are given a voice in the first part of this book, and whose voices are rewritten in the second part, should be thanked: Prof. Rosi Braidotti, Prof. Manuel DeLanda, Prof. Karen Barad, and Prof. Quentin Meillassoux. Our long-distance interview of Prof. Barad at the "7th European Feminist Research Conference" (Utrecht University, June 2009) opened up the idea of the interviews. We would like to thank Heleen Klomp for transcribing the encounter with Prof. Barad, and we would like to thank Prof. Wolfgang Schirmacher (the European Graduate School) for getting us in touch with Prof. Manuel DeLanda. Thank you to Dr. Marie-Pier Boucher for translating the interview with Prof. Quentin Meillassoux and Sterre Ras for formatting the entire book. Also, we would like to thank the editors that run the series "New Metaphysics" at *Open Humanities Press*, Prof. Graham Harman and Prof. Bruno Latour, for their enthusiasm, their support and care, and their inspiring scholarly work that has also been of great influence on this book.

Let us also thank our home institution, the Department of Media and Culture Studies, Faculty of Humanities at Utrecht University, and in particular the Graduate Gender Programme directed by Prof. Rosemarie Buikema, and Media Theory, run by Prof. Joost Raessens. The Research Institute for History and Culture, previously directed by Prof. Maarten Prak and now by Prof. Frank Kessler, and managed by Dr. Frans Ruiter should also be mentioned. Finally, we want to thank Utrecht's Center for the Humanities, run by Prof. Rosi Braidotti, for being our second home and for supporting us in organizing seminars and conferences.

The gust of fresh air that got this whole project started and kept pushing us forward was the Contemporary Cultural Theory (CCT) seminar series that we organized for the past four years. With its more than one hundred seminars, it has created a tremendously rich ecology in which the book was able to flourish. After it started as a reading group for the two of us, it caught the interest of staff members and graduate students and others interested from outside Utrecht University, and it received the generous support of the Centre for the Humanities, Media and Culture Studies, and later the Research Institute for History and Culture. It is impossible to name all those who have shared their valuable thoughts with us in the seminar over the past years, but several of its "usual suspects" have to be named (in no particular order): Marianne van den Boomen, Dr. Birgit Mara Kaiser, Dr. Kathrin Thiele, Nikos Overheul, Dr. Bram Ieven, Beatriz Revelles Benavente, Prof. Frank Kessler, Paulina Bolek, Marietta Radomska, Jannie Pranger, Richard van Meurs, Dr. Nanna Verhoeff, Dr. Paul Bijl, Adinda Veltrop, Freya de Mink, Alex Hebing, Dr. Kees Vuijk, Prof. Paul Ziche, Dr. Kiene Brillenburg Wurth, Prof. Ed Jonker. The seminar series "New Materialism: The Utrecht School" featured our colleagues Prof. Rosi Braidotti, Prof. Maaike Bleeker, Prof. Joost Raessens, Dr. Kathrin Thiele and Dr. Birgit Mara Kaiser.

As part of CCT we had the pleasure to welcome national and international guest speakers (Dr. Marcel Cobussen, Prof. John Protevi, Prof. Rosemarie Buikema, Prof. Gloria Wekker, Dr. Vicki Kirby) and organize conferences. On November 19, 2010 we hosted "Intra-action between the Humanities and the Sciences" with Prof. Rosi Braidotti, Dr. Birgit Mara Kaiser, Jannie Pranger, Prof. Peter Galison, Dr. Fokko Jan Dijksterhuis, Dr. Kathrin Thiele, and Dr. Bibi Straatman. On April 7, 2011 we hosted "New Materialism: Naturecultures" with Prof. Donna

Haraway, Dr. Cecilia Åsberg, Dr. Vicki Kirby, Prof. Rosemarie Buikema, LeineRoebana (Heather Ware and Tim Persent, and Andrea Leine and Harijono Roebana), Dr. Adrian MacKenzie, Dr. Jussi Parikka, Dr. Milla Tiainen, Dr. Melanie Sehgal, and Prof. Rosi Braidotti. The first "New Materialism" conference, organized by Dr. Jussi Parikka and Dr. Milla Tiainen, took place in June 2010 at Anglia Ruskin University/ CoDE in Cambridge, the UK. Our second conference was funded by the Netherlands Organisation for Scientific Research, the Posthumanities Hub (Tema Genus, Linköping University), the Center for the Study of Digital Games and Play, the Graduate Gender Programme, the Center for the Humanities, and the Research Institute for History and Culture (Utrecht University). On November 17, 2011 we organized "Lissitzky Space: New Materialist Experiments" at the Van Abbe Museum (Eindhoven) with Dr. Jondi Keane, Dr. Linda Boersma, Dr. Leslie Kavanaugh, Willem Jan Renders, Annie Fletcher and Piet van de Kar.

Finally we would like to thank our loved ones.

Utrecht, December 2011
Rick Dolphijn and Iris van der Tuin

Introduction
What May I Hope For?

In academia, revolutionary and radical ideas are actualized through an engagement with scholars and scholarly traditions of the canonized past. Contemporary generations read, or more often reread older texts, resulting in "new" readings that do not fit the dominant reception of these texts. Also, academics tend to draw in scholars from an unforeseen past, those who come from a different academic canon or who have been somewhat forgotten. It is in the resonances between old and new readings and re-readings that a "new metaphysics" might announce itself. A new metaphysics is not restricted to a here and now, nor does it merely project an image of the future for us. It announces what we may call a "new tradition," which simultaneously gives us a past, a present, and a future. Thus, a new metaphysics does not add something to thought (a series of ideas that wasn't there, that was left out by others). It rather traverses and thereby rewrites thinking *as a whole*, leaving nothing untouched, redirecting every possible idea according to its new sense of orientation.

"New materialism" or "neo-materialism" is such a new metaphysics. A plethora of contemporary scholars from heterogeneous backgrounds has, since the late 1990s up until now, been producing (re-)readings that together work towards its actualization. This book is written *on* the new materialism simultaneously with its fleshing out *of* the new materialist ambition. The negotiations concerning the new tradition are carried out in the first part of this book. This part consists of four interviews with the most prominent new materialist scholars of today: Rosi Braidotti, Manuel DeLanda, Karen Barad, and Quentin Meillassoux. The second part is made up of four chapters that situate this new tradition in contemporary scholarly thought. The problematics shared by the interviewed scholars are the subject matter of the chapters in Part Two, but it is new materialism that is active everywhere and always throughout. New materialism is the metaphysics that breathes through the entire book, infusing all of its chapters, every statement and argument. New materialism is thus not "built up" in this book: its chapters are not dependent upon one another for understanding their argument. The different chapters of the book can be read independently, although there are many different transversal relations between them.

The interviews in Part One are *intra*-actions rather than *inter*actions. The former term was introduced by Barad and is central to her new materialism. Qualitatively shifting any atomist metaphysics, intra-action conceptualizes that it is the action *between* (and not *in*-between) that matters. In other words, it is not the interviewers or the interviewee or even the oeuvre of the interviewee that deserves our special attention, but it is the sense of orientation that the interview gave rise to (the action itself) that should engender us. For it is in the action itself that new materialism announces itself. We have emphasized this by making strong connections between the individual questions and answers in Part One and the individual chapters of Part Two. This allows the reader to go back and forth between the two parts, in order to gain a deeper understanding of the new materialist tradition.

The interview with Rosi Braidotti revolves, firstly, around the issue of the genealogy of new materialism, and around new materialism as genealogical. The latter can be read either as an instance of Jean-François Lyotard's "rewriting" or of Gilles Deleuze's "creation of concepts." The genealogical element of Braidotti's take on new (feminist) materialism, Braidotti herself being an (un)dutiful daughter of great Continental materialists such as Georges Canguilhem, Michel Foucault and Deleuze (van der Tuin 2009), most certainly pervades the remainder of the book. Braidotti makes clear how it is important to draw situated cartographies of (new) materialisms, and to traverse these maps at the same time in order to produce visionary alternatives, that is, creative alternatives to critique. When it comes to Braidotti's precise take on the matter of materialism, we encounter a

Deleuzean "univocity" or "single matter," while we simultaneously find Braidotti acknowledging difference as a force of sexual differing on the one hand, and a sexual difference that needs to be traversed in order to come up with post-human, post-anthropocentric, and post-secular visions of sustainability and (intergenerational) justice on the other.

The next interview, with Manuel DeLanda, demonstrates how new materialism is indeed filled with a visionary force, and how an attentive study of a material world asks us to look again at notions such as the mind or subjectivity from which this material world is *in*dependent. Braidotti's genealogy comes back in DeLanda's formulation of the new materialism, but initially in the form of dynamic morphogenesis as a historical process that is constitutive *of the material world*. It is only in a secondary instance that DeLanda is interested in the way in which for instance postmodernism or linguisticist idealism has led us away from theorizing scholarly processes as material processes, and as having dynamic, morphogenetic capacities of their own. DeLanda's univocal methodology is at work from the word go, so it could also be argued that the "new" subjectivity or mind, including significant, not signifying, power differences, is always already implied instead of *a priori* established.

In the subsequent interview with Karen Barad, this discussion that cuts across the epistemological and the ontological is continued. For the visionary aspect of a new materialism that she calls "agential realism," Barad brings in a "diffractive" methodology, which is a methodology that allows one to establish the genealogical aspect of Braidotti and the univocity of DeLanda in their entanglement (not interaction). This entanglement comes first, Barad demonstrates via feminist theory and Bohrian quantum physics. She explains how the so-called subject, the so-called instrument, and the so-called object of research are always already entangled, and how measurements are the entanglement of matter and meaning. Barad also singles out the ways in which what she calls "onto-epistemology" is always already *ethical*, that is, how possibilities for post-human agency are part of what Braidotti would call (sexual) differing, and what DeLanda would call morphogenesis. All of this opens up for a notion of matter that, as Barad says in the interview, affirms that matter "feels, converses, suffers, desires, yearns, and remembers" because "feeling, desiring and experiencing are not singular characteristics or capacities of human consciousness."

The final interview with Quentin Meillassoux seems to go back to the new materialism proposed by DeLanda. Whereas Barad and Braidotti work towards a new materialism that is immediately ontological, epistemological, and ethical, DeLanda and Meillassoux seem to be more interested in the ontological, either at the expense of an immediate or simultaneous interest in epistemology and ethics (DeLanda) or by leading up to epistemological questions of the classificatory kind (Meillassoux). This reading, however, would itself be classificatory, and would divide the terrain to an extent that may overstate differences and overlook similarities. Meillassoux produces a new materialism (a "speculative materialism") that radicalizes the relation between epistemology and ontology, thus producing a new materialism that can access the in-itself. Similar to the projects of the three other interviewees, it is especially a subjectivism (also known as a social constructivism, a linguistic idealism, or an identity politics) that is qualitatively shifted in the anti-anthropocentric work of Meillassoux. Here, a "realism" is brought forward that intends to do justice to matter and the contingency of nature most radically, while stressing the limitlessness of thought.

In terms of academic attention, new materialism is in many ways a wave approaching its crest. The amount of publications on this topic is growing, especially in cultural and feminist theory (see e.g. Alaimo and Hekman eds. 2008; Coole and Frost eds. 2010; Bolt and Barrett eds. forthcoming). As the authors of this book we have engaged actively in the constitution and application of new materialism (e.g. Dolphijn 2004; van der Tuin 2008; Dolphijn 2011; van der Tuin 2011). With this book, which is the result of an intense cooperation over several years, we have aimed at producing an open cartography of new materialism that radically explores this new tradition in thought, and that aims at including all that it can virtually do.

I
Interviews

Chapter 1
"The notion of the univocity of Being or single matter positions difference as a verb or process of becoming at the heart of the matter"
Interview with Rosi Braidotti

Q1: In your contribution to Ian Buchanan and Claire Colebrook's Deleuze and Feminist Theory *you coined the term "neo-materialism" and provided a genealogy of it. Focusing on theories of the subject, one of the red threads running through your work, your genealogy "Descartes' nightmare, Spinoza's hope, Nietzsche's complaint, Freud's obsession, Lacan's favorite fantasy" (Braidotti 2000, 159) is followed by a definition of the subject, the "I think" as the body of which it is an idea, which we see as the emblem of the new materialism:*

> *A piece of meat activated by electric waves of desire, a text written by the unfolding of genetic encoding. Neither a sacralised inner* sanctum, *nor a pure socially shaped entity, the enfleshed Deleuzian subject is rather an 'in-between': it is a folding-in of external influences and a simultaneous unfolding outwards of affects. A mobile entity, an enfleshed sort of memory that repeats and is capable of lasting through sets of discontinuous variations, while remaining faithful to itself. The Deleuzian body is ultimately an embodied memory (ibid.).*

In this text you stay close to the philosophy of Gilles Deleuze when developing the new materialism. The term, however, can already be found in Patterns of Dissonance, *where you state that "a general direction of thought is emerging in feminist theory that situates the embodied nature of the subject, and consequently the question of alternatively sexual difference or gender, at the heart of matter. [...] This leads to a radical re-reading of materialism, away from its strictly Marxist definition. [...] The neo-materialism of Foucault, the new materiality proposed by Deleuze are [...] a point of no return for feminist theory" (Braidotti 1991, 263–6), and in* Nomadic Subjects *where it is stated that "What emerges in poststructuralist feminist reaffirmations of difference is [...] a new materialist theory of the text and of textual practice" (Braidotti 1994, 154). How is "genealogy" important for you, and how is it that the full-fledged conceptualization of the new materialism came about in a text that focused on the philosophy of Deleuze?*

Rosi Braidotti: You're right in pointing out the progressive development of and identification with the label "neo-materialism" within the corpus of my nomadic thought. *Patterns of Dissonance* announces my general project outline in theoretical terms, which are expressed in the mainstream language that is typical of book versions of former PhD dissertations. Then there follows a trilogy, composed by *Nomadic Subjects, Metamorphoses* and *Transpositions. Nomadic Subjects*—which incidentally has just been re-issued by Columbia University Press in a totally revised second edition seventeen years after its original publication (Braidotti 2011b)—already has a more controversial message and a more upbeat style. *Metamorphoses* and *Transpositions* pursue the experiment in a conceptual structure that has grown more complex and rhizomatic and a style that attempts to do justice to this complexity, while not losing touch with the readers altogether.

More theoretically, I would argue that, throughout the 1980's, a text such as Althusser's "Pour un matérialisme aléatoire" had established a consensus across the whole spectrum of his students—Foucault, Deleuze, Balibar. It was clear that contemporary materialism had to be redefined in the light of recent scientific insights, notably psychoanalysis, but also in terms of the critical enquiry into the mutations of advanced capitalism. It was understood that the post-'68 thinkers had to be simultaneously loyal to the Marxist legacy, but also critical and creative in adapting it to the fast-changing conditions of their historicity. That theoretico-political consensus made the term "materialist" both a necessity and a banality for some poststructuralists. Leading figures in the linguistic turn, such as Barthes and Lacan, wrote extensively and frequently about "the materiality of the sign." In a way there was no real need to add the prefix "neo-" to the new materialist consensus at that point in time. That, however, will change.

What is clear is that by the mid-1990's the differences among the various strands and branches of the post-structuralist project were becoming more explicit. The hegemonic position acquired by the linguistic branch—developed via psychoanalysis and semiotics into a fully-fledged deconstructive project that simply conquered intellectually the United States—intensified the need for clearer terms of demarcation and of theoretical definition. Thus "neo-materialism" emerges as a method, a conceptual frame and a political stand, which refuses the linguistic paradigm, stressing instead the concrete yet complex materiality of bodies immersed in social relations of power.

At that point, it became clear to me that the genealogical line that connected me to Canguilhem, Foucault and Deleuze also marked a distinctive tradition of thought on issues of embodiment and political subjectivity. The terminological differences between this branch and the deconstructive one also became sharper, as did the political priorities. Accordingly, "nomadic subjects" is neither about representation nor about recognition but rather about expression and actualization of practical alternatives. Gilles Deleuze—from his (smoky) seminar room at Vincennes—provided lucid and illuminating guidance to those involved in the project of redefining what exactly is the "matter" that neo-materialism is made of. Things get more conceptually rigorous from that moment on.

Feminism, of course, did more than its share. Feminist philosophy builds on the embodied and embedded brand of materialism that was pioneered in the last century by Simone de Beauvoir. It combines, in a complex and groundbreaking manner, phenomenological theory of embodiment with Marxist—and later on poststructuralist—re-elaborations of the complex intersection between bodies and power. This rich legacy has two long-lasting theoretical consequences. The first is that feminist philosophy goes even further than mainstream continental philosophy in rejecting dualistic partitions of minds from bodies or nature from culture. Whereas the chasm between the binary oppositions is bridged by Anglo-American gender theorists through dynamic schemes of social constructivism (Butler and

Scott eds. 1992), continental feminist perspectives move towards either theories of sexual difference or a monistic political ontology that makes the sex/gender distinction redundant.

The second consequence of this specific brand of materialism is that oppositional consciousness combines critique with creativity, in a "double-edged vision" (Kelly 1979) that does not stop at critical deconstruction but moves on to the active production of alternatives. Thus, feminist philosophers have introduced a new brand of materialism, of the embodied and embedded kind. The cornerstone of this theoretical innovation is a specific brand of situated epistemology (Haraway 1988), which evolves from the practice of "the politics of location" (Rich 1985) and infuses standpoint feminist theory and the debates with postmodernist feminism (Harding 1991) throughout the 1990s.

As a meta-methodological innovation, the embodied and embedded brand of feminist materialist philosophy of the subject introduces a break from both universalism and dualism. As for the former, universalist claims to a subject position that allegedly transcends spatio-temporal and geo-political specificities are criticised for being dis-embodied and dis-embedded, i.e., abstract. Universalism, best exemplified in the notion of "abstract masculinity" (Hartsock 1987) and triumphant whiteness (Ware 1992), is objectionable not only on epistemological, but also on ethical grounds. Situated perspectives lay the pre-conditions for ethical accountability for one's own implications with the very structures one is analyzing and opposing politically. The key concept in feminist materialism is the sexualized nature and the radical immanence of power relations and their effects upon the world. In this Foucauldian perspective, power is not only negative or confining (*potestas*), but also affirmative (*potentia*) or productive of alternative subject positions and social relations.

Feminist anti-humanism, also known as postmodern feminism, expanded on the basic critique of one-sided universalism, while pointing out the dangers implicit in a flat application of equal opportunities policies. Contrary to "standpoint theory" (Harding 1986), post-humanist feminist philosophers do not unquestionably rely on the notion of "difference," as the dialectical motor of social change. They rather add more complexity to this debate by analyzing the ways in which "otherness" and "sameness" interact in an asymmetrical set of power relations. This is analogous to Deleuze's theories of Otherness; his emphasis on processes, dynamic interaction and fluid boundaries is a materialist, high-tech brand of vitalism, which makes Deleuze's thought highly relevant to the analysis of the late industrialist patriarchal culture we inhabit. Furthermore, Deleuze's work is of high relevance for feminism: not only does he display a great empathy with issues of difference, sexuality and transformation, but he also invests the site of the feminine with positive force. Conveyed by figurations such as the non-Oedipal Alice: the little girl about to be dispossessed of her body by the Oedipal Law, or by the more affirmative figure of the philosopher's fiancée Ariadne, the feminine face of philosophy is one of the sources of the transmutation of values from negative into affirmative. This metamorphosis allows Deleuze to overcome the boundaries that separate mere critique from active empowerment. Last but not least, Deleuze's emphasis on the "becoming woman" of philosophy marks a new kind of masculine style of philosophy: it is a philosophical sensibility which has learned to undo the straitjacket of phallocentrism and to take a few risks. In Deleuze's thought, the "other" is not the emblematic and invariably vampirized mark of alterity, as in classical philosophy. Nor is it a fetishized and necessarily othered "other," as in deconstruction. It is a moving horizon of exchanges and becoming, towards which the non-unitary subjects of postmodernity move, are by which they are moved in return.

This double genealogy makes my own relationship to materialism into a lifelong engagement with complexities and inner contradictions.

Q2: In the same chapter in Deleuze and Feminist Theory *the new materialism is also called "anti-maternalist" (Braidotti 2000, 172). Maternal feminism surely is, along with feminist standpoint theory, a feminist materialism. So, on the menu we find "the naturalistic paradigm" and its "definitive loss" (ibid., 158), feminist materialisms, "social constructivism" (ibid.), and, finally, "a more radical sense of materialism" (ibid., 161), that is, an "anti-essentialism" (ibid., 158), "a form of neo-materialism and a blend of vitalism that is attuned to the technological era" (ibid., 160). In* Metamorphoses *you propose a cartographical method for contemporary philosophical dialogue according to which "we think of power-relations simultaneously as the most 'external', collective, social phenomenon and also as the most intimate or 'internal' one" (Braidotti 2002a, 6). Looking back at your chapter in* Deleuze and Feminist Theory, *how would you employ this method to draw a contemporary map of the new feminist materialist dialogue? Or, from a slightly different angle, your chapter from* Patterns of Dissonance *on the radical philosophies of sexual difference (a branch of feminist theory that does not necessarily overlap with the trademarked "French feminism" and which is very much a materialism) closes with the provocative question: "have they been heard?" (Braidotti 1991, 273). How would you answer your 1991 question nowadays, amidst the theorizations of new feminist materialisms?*

RB: The issue of the relationship between the material and the maternal was crucial for my generation. Part of it was contextual: we were the first ones in fact to enjoy the privilege of having strong, feminist teachers and supervisors in our academic work. In my case, I had as teachers and role models women of the caliber of Genevieve Lloyd and Luce Irigaray, Michelle Perrot and Joan Scott—to mention just the major ones. Talk about the anxiety of influence! This sort of lineage made the issue of the oedipalization of the pedagogical relationship into a crucial and complicated matter. Another reason for it was of course theoretical: if you look back at the scholarship of the 1980s, you will find a plethora of texts and treatises on pedagogics and mother-daughter relationships. Psychoanalysis alone blew this issue out of all proportions, and with the privilege of hindsight you may say that the entire post-1968 generation has a big negative relation to their mothers and fathers. I guess all members of a revolutionary generation are marked by the violence of a break, an inevitable rupture from the previous generation.

Personally, I fast grew allergic to the whole oedipal theme, also because I witnessed the many violent and sharp conflicts it engendered in the feminist community—the clash between Cixous and de Beauvoir being a legendary one. In some ways I was scared of the negative passions that the "maternal" mobilized in a highly politicized context. I consequently took shelter in the first volume of *Capitalism and Schizophrenia*, aptly called *Anti-Oedipus*, and made sure to apply it to the question of how to develop an independent yet loyal system of thought in relation to the development of feminist philosophy. This choice coincided with my decision to bring feminism into the institutions, which I took as a process of democratic accountability. Central to it, of course, is the project of inter-generational justice.

All of my cartographies are as inclusive as I'm capable of making them and I've carefully avoided sectarianism, while taking a firm theoretical and political stand (Braidotti 2010). This standpoint was also for me a way of staying sane through the multiple "theory wars" and "culture wars" we witnessed through the 1990's, as the right wing took over the agenda in the USA and the post-1989 global consensus tends to dismiss the key traditions of thought I consider as fundamental for my work: Marxist and post-structuralist theories of materialism.

Right now there is a need for a systematic meta-discursive approach to the interdisciplinary methods of feminist philosophy. This is among the top priorities for philosophy today (Alcoff 2000) as well as women's, gender and feminist studies as an established discipline (Wiegman 2002). If it is the case that what was once subversive is now mainstream, it follows that the challenge for feminist philosophers today is how to hold their position, while striving to achieve more conceptual creativity (Deleuze and Guattari [1991] 1994).

In a globally connected and technologically mediated world that is marked by rapid changes, structural inequalities and increased militarization, feminist scholarship has intensified theoretical and methodological efforts to come to grips with the complexities of the present, while resisting the moral and cognitive panic that marks so much of contemporary social theories of globalization (Fukuyama 2002, Habermas 2003). With the demise of postmodernism, which has gone down in history as a form of radical scepticism and moral and cognitive relativism, feminist philosophers tend to move beyond the linguistic mediation paradigm of deconstructive theory and to work instead towards the production of robust alternatives. Issues of embodiment and accountability, positionality and location have become both more relevant and more diverse. My main argument is that feminist philosophy is currently finding a new course between post-humanism on the one hand and post-anthropocentric theories on the other. The convergence between these two approaches, multiplied across the many inter-disciplinary lines that structure feminist theory, ends up radicalizing the very premises of feminist philosophy. It results especially in a reconsideration of the priority of sexuality and the relevance of the sex/gender distinction.

It is more difficult to answer the question of whether the radical philosophies of sexual difference, as a form of neo-materialism that doesn't necessarily overlap with French feminism (a misnomer on many accounts) had actually been heard. The paradigmatic status of the sex/gender distinction in American feminist theory and the global reach of this paradigm, for instance across the former Eastern Europe after 1989, has made it difficult for situated European perspectives to keep alive, let alone move forth.

Most notably, this sex/gender distinction has become the core of the so-called "Trans-Atlantic dis-connection." If I were to attempt to translate this into the language of feminist theory, I would say that "the body" in U.S. feminism cannot be positively associated with sexuality in either the critical or the public discourse. Sexuality, which is the fundamental paradigm in the critical discourses of psychoanalysis and post-structuralism, simply has no place to be in American political discourse: it got strangled. What chance, then, did "French feminism" have? The sex/gender dichotomy swung towards the pole of gender with a vengeance, disembodying it under the joint cover of liberal individual "rights" and social constructivist "change." It was left to the gay and lesbian and queer campaigners to try to reverse this trend, rewriting sexuality into the feminist agenda. For instance, Teresa de Lauretis (1994) returns to issues of psychoanalytic desire in order to provide a foundational theory of lesbian identity. Judith Butler reverses the order of priorities in the sex/gender dichotomy in favor of the former and manages to combine Foucault with Wittig. By now, observers begin to speak of American post-structuralism as a movement of its own, with its own specific features and conceptual aims. The fact that most leading French poststructuralists take up regular teaching positions in the USA favors this second life of post-structuralism, which in the meantime dies away in Europe and disappears especially from the French intellectual scene. By the start of the third millennium, "French" theory belongs to the world in a diasporic, not a universalist mode. The Frenchness of post-structuralism is lost in translation indeed, just as it undergoes a conceptual mutation in the Trans-Atlantic transition.

One practical action I took in order to make sure that other, more European approaches were heard is to set up EU-wide networks of women's gender and feminist studies, of which ATHENA (the Advanced Thematic Network of Women's Studies in Europe) is the best example. Theoretically, my function as ATHENA founding director resulted in friendly but firm criticism of American hegemony in feminist theory and an attempt to develop other perspectives, drawn from historical and situated European traditions. I think we've been heard, insofar as counter-memories and alternative genealogies can ever be heard. The sheer tone and structure of this interview with you—a younger generation of critical thinkers—gives me great reason to rejoice and feel a renewed hope.

Q3: Your philosophy has always been a philosophy of difference. *In the chapter "Sexual Difference as a Nomadic Political Project" from* Nomadic Subjects (1994) *you explain why, and follow Luce Irigaray doing so. First, you claim to attempt to shift difference-as-a-dialectics, which underpins Western, Eurocentric thought. Here, "in this history," you claim, "difference" has been predicated on relations of domination and exclusion, to be "different-from" came to mean to be "less than," to* be worth *less than" (Braidotti 1994, 147; original emphasis). Second, you try to break through the canon of Western feminism, which has dismissed sexual difference "in the name of a polemical form of "antiessentialism," or of a utopian longing for a position "beyond gender," (ibid., 149). Developing your own approach, you have consistently focused on "sexual difference as a project," as a "nomadic political project" (ibid.). Doing so, you have relied on so-called "French feminism" and "French theory."*

Having discussed "French feminism" and its place in contemporary academia in question 2, what is your take on French theory at large in contemporary academia? Apart from its canonical version, which has been created in an Anglo-U.S. context just like "French feminism," do you see minor traditions in academia that are equally "French"? And if so, how do they look and how are they related to the new materialism?

RB: It is clear by now that we need to deterritorialize French theory in order to rescue it from the debacle it suffered in North America. This is a double challenge, considering how right-wing the European intellectual context has become in the last decade. A further factor that delays the development of situated European perspectives is the perennial hostility between French and German philosophical traditions. There are however three main points worth stressing: first, a tendency to move beyond the analytic versus Continental divide in philosophy, as indicated by John Mullarkey (2006) in his work on "post-continental" philosophy. German philosopher Dieter Thomä makes a similar case in the volume I edited for the *History of Continental Philosophy* (Braidotti ed. 2010). These are encouraging developments that allow us to activate new theoretical and methodological resources within the previously antagonistic traditions.

Second, the productive contribution of radical epistemologies to the reception of French philosophy also needs to be stressed. Nowadays, there can be no reading of Canguilhem without taking into account Haraway's work; no Derrida without Butler or Spivak; no Foucault without Stuart Hall and no Deleuze without materialist feminists. This is a point of no return.

Third, to address more directly your question I think French philosophy is rich in minor traditions, which we would do well to revisit. They range from the less globally recognized, but nonetheless quintessentially French tradition of philosophy of science and epistemology to the emphasis on sexuality of the libertine tradition. My personal favorite is the enchanted materialism of Diderot and an established tradition that links rationalism directly to the imagination. They are a multiplicity of mountain streams that converge upon mainstream materialism.

Q4: Do you agree that difference is quintessential to the new materialism? And if so, how would you define its take on difference?

RB: Absolutely—especially if one follows Deleuze on this point and posits monism as the fundamental ontology. The notion of the univocity of Being or single matter positions difference as a verb or process of becoming at the heart of that matter. There are only variations or modulations of space and time within a common block so it's all about patterns of repetition and difference. Within such a system of thought, moreover, sexual difference plays a crucial role.

Sexual difference in particular poses the question of the conditions of possibility for thought as a self-originating system of representation of itself as the ultimate presence. Thus, sexual difference produces subjectivity in general. The conceptual tool by which Irigaray had already shown this peculiar logic is the notion of "the sensible transcendental." By showing that what is erased in the process of erection of the transcendental subject are the maternal grounds of origin, Irigaray simultaneously demystifies the vertical transcendence of the subject and calls for an alternative metaphysics. Irigaray's transcendental is sensible and grounded in the very particular fact that all human life is, for the time being, still "of woman born" (Rich 1976). There are resonances between the early Irigaray and Deleuze's work.

As I have often argued, Deleuze's emphasis on the productive and positive force of difference is troublesome for feminist theory in so far as it challenges the foundational value of sexual difference. For Irigaray, on the other hand, the metaphysical question of sexual difference is the horizon of feminist theory; for Grosz ([1993] 1994) it is even its precondition. For Butler (1993) difference is a problem to overcome, as a limit of the discourse of embodiment; for me however sexual difference is the situated corporeal location that one starts from—it is a negotiable, transversal, affective space. The advantage of a Deleuzian as well as Irigarayan approach is that the emphasis shifts from the metaphysics to the ethics of sexual difference. Deleuze's brand of philosophical pragmatism questions whether sexual difference demands metaphysics at all. The distinctive traits of nomadic sexual difference theory is that difference is not taken as a problem to solve, or an obstacle to overcome, but rather as a fact and a factor of our situated, corporeal location. And it is not a prerogative only of humans, either. This has important methodological consequences.

Following Deleuze's empiricism, Colebrook for instance wants to shift the grounds of the debate away from metaphysical foundations to a philosophy of immanence that stresses the need to create new concepts. This creative gesture is a way of responding to the given, to experience, and is thus linked to the notion of the event. The creation of concepts is itself experience or experimentation. There is a double implication here: firstly that philosophy need not be seen as the master discourse or the unavoidable horizon of thought: artistic and scientific practices have their role to play as well. Secondly, given that ethical questions do not require metaphysics, the feminist engagement with concepts need not be critical but can be inventive and creative. In other words, experimenting with thinking is what we all need to learn. That implies the de-territorialization of the very sexual difference we started off from.

Q5: In your recent work you focus on "post-humanism" and "post-secularism." In two articles in Theory, Culture and Society *you elaborate on both terms. In fact, you immediately complexify the post-human by weaving a post-anthropocentrism through it, which is an intervention ascribed to feminist theory: "The feminist post-anthropocentric approach [...] also challenges the androcentrism of the post-structuralists' corporeal materialism" (Braidotti 2006, 198). In addition, you claim that for instance Donna Haraway's post-anthropocentric post-humanism is not an anti-foundationalism; it is a "process ontology" instead (ibid., 199). Apart from the fact that you capitalize on Haraway's Whiteheadian moment here ("Beings do not pre-exist their relatings" (Haraway 2003, 6)), you also ascribe a specific theory of time to feminist post-humanism, a theory that seems Bergsonian:*

> To be in process or transition does not place the thinking subject outside history or time [...]. A location is an embedded and embodied memory: it is a set of counter-memories, which are activated by the resisting thinker against the grain of the dominant representations of subjectivity. A location is a materialist temporal and spatial site of co-production of the subject, and thus anything but an instance of relativism (Braidotti 2006, 199).

Process ontology, along with neo-vitalism, also provides the key to your conceptualization of the post-secular, albeit that sticking to the psychoanalytic frame remains of importance to you (Braidotti 2008, 12–13). In your work, post-secularism is conceptualized as follows:

> The post secular position on the affirmative force of oppositional consciousness inevitably raises the question of faith in possible futures, which is one of the aspects of [...] residual spirituality [...]. Faith in progress itself is a vote of confidence in the future. Ultimately, it is a belief in the perfectibility of Wo/Man, albeit it in a much more grounded, accountable mode that privileges partial perspectives, as Haraway (1988) put it. It is a post secular position in that it is an immanent, not transcendental theory, which posits generous bonds of cosmopolitanism, solidarity and community across locations and generations. It also expresses sizeable doses of residual spirituality in its yearning for social justice and sustainability (ibid., 18).

In your view, the post-secular is thus intrinsic to contemporary feminist theories of difference, perceived as structured by a politics of affirmation rather than negation or dialectics (ibid., 13). And once more, theory's non-linear temporality, in its Whiteheadian as well as Bergsonian mode, appears to be key.

In your theorization of the post-secular, however, the strong anti-androcentric approach of feminist theory seems to disappear somewhat, albeit that process ontology and neo-vitalism are explicited. How is post-secular feminism an anti-androcentrism? How, for instance, should we conceptualize this faith in "the perfectibility of Wo/Man"?

RB: My starting assumption is that the post-secular turn challenges European political theory in general and feminism in particular because it makes manifest the notion that agency, or political subjectivity, can actually be conveyed through and supported by religious piety and may even involve significant amounts of spirituality. This statement has an important corollary—namely, that political agency need not be critical in the negative sense of oppositional and thus may not be aimed solely or primarily at the production of counter-subjectivities. Subjectivity is rather a process ontology of auto-poiesis or self-styling, which involves complex and continuous negotiations with dominant norms and values and hence also multiple forms of accountability. This position is defended within feminism by a variety of different thinkers ranging from Harding and Narayan (2000) to Mahmood (2005).

The corollary of this axiom is the belief that women's emancipation is directly indexed upon sexual freedom, in keeping with the European liberal tradition of individual rights and self-autonomy. As Joan Scott (2007) recently argued, this historically specific model cannot be universalized and it is the basic fault of contemporary European politicians that they enforced this model and insist on its homogeneity in spite of rising evidence of its contingent and hence partial applicability. This is a crucial point, which again stresses the importance of sexuality as the major axis of subject-formation in European culture and in its philosophies of subjectivity. It is precisely because of the historical importance of sexuality that sexual difference is such a central axis in the formation of identity and of social relations.

Thus the post-secular predicament forces, if not a complete revision, at least a relativization of the dominant European paradigm that equates emancipation with sexual liberation. Moreover, the post-secular position on the affirmative force of oppositional consciousness inevitably raises the question of the desire for and faith in possible futures, which is one of the aspects of the residual spirituality I mentioned above. The system of feminist civic values rests on a social constructivist notion of faith as the hope for the construction of alternative social horizons, new norms and values. Faith in progress itself is a vote of confidence in the future. Ultimately, it is a belief in the perfectibility of Wo/Man, albeit it in a much more grounded, accountable mode that privileges partial perspectives, as Haraway (1988) put it.

Desire is never a given. Rather, like a long shadow projected from the past, it is a forward-moving horizon that lies ahead and towards which one moves. Between the "no longer" and the "not yet," desire traces the possible patterns of becoming. These intersect with and mobilize sexuality, but only to deterritorialize the parameters of a gender system that today more than ever combines redemptive emancipatory benevolence with violent militarized coercion into the Western neo-imperial project. Against the platitudes of sex as conspicuous consumption and the arrogance of nationalist projects of enforced liberation of non-Westerners, critical thinkers today may want to re-think sexuality beyond genders, as the ontological drive to pure becoming. Desire sketches the conditions for intersubjective encounters between the no longer and the not yet, through the unavoidable accident of an insight, a flush of sudden acceleration that marks a point of non-return. Accepting the challenge of de-territorialized nomadic sexuality may rescue contemporary sexual politics from the paradoxical mix of commercialized banalities and perennial counter-identity claims on the one hand, and belligerent and racist forms of neo-colonial civilizationism on the other.

Q6: As a final experiment, let us try to move feminism beyond ideas about the social and cultural embeddedness of embodied femininity by discussing the way in which you work with the notion of the nomad. In Difference and Repetition *Deleuze ([1968] 1994, 36) already contrasted the nomad to* nomos, *and it seems that throughout your work you delve into this particular opposition more and more. In other words, it seems to be interested increasingly not so much in a feminism that is about a rethinking of the relation between the female and the male, or the relation between the female and the world, what is at stake in your feminism is* *thinking about "woman" in all of its morphogenetic and topological virtualities. From the "other materialism" which you already propose in the final chapter of your first book (*Patterns of Dissonance*) in 1991 to claims like "Language is a virus" (in* Nomadic Subjects*), you have already pushed feminism way beyond the idea that the female should be thought as "the Other" and even beyond Deleuze and Guattari's "becoming-woman" which in some way comes close to a nomadology but still implies the social and cultural relationality which the nomad does not need. Could we conclude (with Arnold Toynbee) that the nomad is she who "does not move" but is merely interested in the experimenting and experiencing femininity in all its material realizations? Or better, has the concept of the nomad allowed you to set in motion a return to a radical Spinozism that studies not so much the social and cultural aspects of feminism, but simply poses the question* what a woman can do*?*

RB: What a great question! I wish we could run a six-week seminar on it! The starting point for most feminist redefinitions of subjectivity is a new form of materialism that develops the notion of corporeal materiality by emphasizing the embodied and therefore sexually differentiated structure of the speaking subject. Consequently, rethinking the bodily roots of subjectivity is the starting point for the epistemological project of nomadism. The body or the embodiment of the subject is to be understood as neither a biological nor a sociological category, but rather as a point of overlap between the physical, the symbolic, and the sociological. I stress the issue of embodiment so as to make a plea for different ways of thinking about the body. The body refers to the materialist but also vitalist groundings of human subjectivity and to the specifically human capacity to be both grounded and to flow and thus to transcend the very variables—class, race, sex, gender, age, disability—which structure us. It rests on a post-identitarian view of what constitutes a subject.

A nomadic vision of the body defines it as multi-functional and complex, as a transformer of flows and energies, affects, desires and imaginings. From psychoanalysis I have learned to appreciate the advantages of the non-unitary structure of the subject and the joyful implication of the unconscious foundations of the subject. Complexity is the key term for understanding the multiple affective layers, the complex temporal variables and the internally contradictory time- and memory-lines that frame our embodied existence. In contrast with the oppositions created by dualistic modes of social constructivism, a nomadic body is a threshold of transformations. It is the complex interplay of the highly constructed social and symbolic forces. The body is a surface of intensities and an affective field in interaction with others. In other words, feminist emphasis on embodiment goes hand-in-hand with a radical rejection of essentialism. In feminist theory one *speaks as* a woman, although the subject "woman" is not a monolithic essence defined once and for all, but rather the site of multiple, complex, and potentially contradictory sets of experiences, defined by overlapping variables, such as class, race, age, life-style, sexual preference and others. One speaks as a woman in order to empower women, to activate socio-symbolic changes in their condition; this is a radically anti-essentialist position.

The nomad expresses my own figuration of a situated, postmodern, culturally differentiated understanding of the subject in general and of the feminist subject in particular. This subject can also be described as postmodern/postindustrial/postcolonial, depending on one's location. In so far as axes of differentiation like class, race, ethnicity, gender, age and others intersect and interact with each other in the constitution of subjectivity, the notion of nomad refers to the simultaneous occurrence of many of these at once. Speaking as a feminist entails that priority is granted to issues of gender (or rather, of sexual difference) in connection with the recognition of differences among women. This figuration translates therefore my desire to explore and legitimate political agency, while taking as historical evidence the decline of metaphysically fixed, steady identities. One of the issues at stake here is how to reconcile partiality and discontinuity with the construction of new forms of inter-relatedness and collective political projects.

The political strategy doubles up as a methodology; transformative projects involve a radical repositioning on the part of the knowing subject, which is neither self-evident nor free from pain. No process of consciousness-raising ever is. In post-structuralist feminism, the "alternative science project" (Harding 1986) has also been implemented methodologically through the practice of dis-identification from familiar and hence comforting values and identities (De Lauretis 1986, Braidotti 1994).

Dis-identification involves the loss of cherished habits of thought and representation, a move that can also produce fear and a sense of insecurity and nostalgia. Change is certainly a painful process, but this does not equate it with suffering, nor does it warrant the politically conservative position that chastises all change as dangerous. The point in stressing the difficulties and pain involved in the quest for transformative processes is rather to raise an awareness of both the complexities involved, the paradoxes that lie in store and to develop a nomadic "ethics of compassion" (Connolly 1999).

Changes that affect one's sense of identity are especially delicate. Given that identifications constitute an inner scaffolding that supports one's sense of identity, shifting our imaginary identifications is not as simple as casting away a used garment. Psychoanalysis taught us that imaginary re-locations are complex, and as time-consuming as shedding an old skin. Moreover, changes of this qualitative kind happen more easily at the molecular or subjective level, and their translation into a public discourse and shared social experiences is a complex and risk-ridden affair. In a more positive vein, Spinozist feminist political thinkers like Moira Gatens and Genevieve Lloyd (1999) argue that such socially embedded and historically grounded changes are the result of "collective imaginings"—a shared desire for certain transformations to be actualised as a collaborative effort. They are transversal assemblages aimed at the production of affirmative politics and ethical relations.

De-familiarization is a sobering process by which the knowing subject evolves from the normative vision of the self he or she had become accustomed to. The frame of reference becomes the open-ended, interrelational, multi-sexed, and trans-species flows of becoming by interaction with multiple others. A subject thus constituted explodes the boundaries of humanism at skin level.

However, as Irigaray teaches us, changing the boundaries of what a woman can do entails the shift of fundamental parameters. Ontologically, in terms of the spatio-temporal frame of becoming; symbolically, through liturgies of actualization and the formalization of adequate modes of expression; and socially, in practical forms of collaborative morality and transitional politics that may lead to a more radical form of democracy. As I argued earlier, the conditions for renewed political and ethical agency cannot be drawn from the immediate context or the current state of the terrain. They have to be generated affirmatively and creatively by efforts geared to creating possible futures, by mobilizing resources and visions that have been left untapped and by actualizing them in daily practices of interconnection with others.

This project requires more visionary power or prophetic energy, qualities which are neither especially in fashion in academic circles, nor highly valued scientifically in these times of commercial globalization. Yet, the call for more vision is emerging from many quarters in critical theory. Feminists have a long and rich genealogy in terms of pleading for increased visionary insight. From the very early days, Joan Kelly (1979) typified feminist theory as a double-edged vision, with a strong critical and an equally strong creative function. Faith in the creative powers of the imagination is an integral part of feminists' appraisal of lived embodied experience and the bodily roots of subjectivity, which would express the complex singularities that feminist women have become. Donna Haraway's work (1997, 2003) provides the best example of this kind of respect for a dimension where creativity is unimaginable without some visionary fuel.

Prophetic or visionary minds are thinkers of the future. The future as an active object of desire propels us forth and motivates us to be active in the here and now of a continuous present that calls for resistance. The yearning for sustainable futures can construct a liveable present. This is not a leap of faith, but an active transposition, a transformation at the in-depth level (Braidotti 2006). A prophetic or visionary dimension is necessary in order to secure an affirmative hold over the present, as the launching pad for sustainable becoming or qualitative transformations. The future is the virtual unfolding of the affirmative aspect of the present, which honours our obligations to the generations to come.

The pursuit of practices of hope, rooted in the ordinary micro-practices of everyday life, is a simple strategy to hold, sustain and map out sustainable transformations. The motivation for the social construction of hope is grounded in a profound sense of responsibility and accountability. A fundamental gratuitousness and a profound sense of hope is part of it. Hope is a way of dreaming up possible futures, an anticipatory virtue that permeates our lives and activates them. It is a powerful motivating force grounded not only in projects that aim at reconstructing the social imaginary, but also in the political economy of desires, affects and creativity. Contemporary nomadic practices of subjectivity—both in pedagogy and other areas of thought—work towards a more affirmative approach to critical theory.

Chapter 2
"Any materialist philosophy must take as its point of departure the existence of a material world that is independent of our minds"
Interview with Manuel DeLanda

Q1: In your short text "The Geology of Morals, A Neo-Materialist Interpretation" from 1996 you introduce the term "neo-materialism" rewriting the way in which Deleuze and Guattari, in their A Thousand Plateaus *([1980] 1987), use Hjelmslev's linguistic model (which according to Deleuze and Guattari thus goes far beyond the reach of language) of form, content, substance and expression in order to conceptualize geological movements. In your reading of it, you make no use of Hjelmslev but instead favor other concepts like strata, deterritorialization and reterritorialization in order to map the morphogenetic changes of the real. There is no reason why neo-materialism should make use of particular concepts (like the ones mentioned) or even of particular authors like Hjelmslev. Yet what seems to be crucial for it would be to revitalize an interest in an affirmative reading of the dynamics among processes of materialization, as it offers us a thinking which starts with "bodily motions alone," as Spinoza would put it ([1677] 2001, E2P49 Schol.) and how this allows us to rethink very different branches of academia such as geology, mathematics, cultural theory, (neo-classical) economics and sociology.*

In your book Intensive Science and Virtual Philosophy *from 2002 you give a beautiful definition of what 'a history' is, which made us rethink the way in which new materialism could be situated in academic thought. You write,*

> The well-defined nature of the possible histories is not to be approached by a mere mention of laws expressed as differential

> equations, but by an understanding of how such equations in fact
> individuate trajectories (DeLanda 2002, 36).

Can we conclude that the books you wrote and the way in which your new materialist arguments rewrite the various branches of academia, are all about the creation of such "individuated trajectories" that invent *a neo-materialism? In other words, could we even say that your neo-materialism, though inspired by Deleuze and Braudel, cannot even be said to have these authors as its point of departure?*

Manuel DeLanda: Any materialist philosophy must take as its point of departure the existence of a material world that is independent of our minds. But then it confronts the problem of the origin of the enduring identity of the inhabitants of that world: if the mind is not what gives identity to mountains and rivers, plants and animals, then what does? An old answer is "essences," the answer given by Aristotle. But if one rejects essentialism then there is no choice but to answer the question like this: all objective entities are products of a historical process, that is, their identity is synthesized or produced as part of cosmological, geological, biological, or social history. This need for a concept of "synthesis" or of "production" is what attracted Marx to Hegelian dialectics since it provided him with a model of synthesis: a conflict of opposites or the negation of the negation. Deleuze and Guattari, on the other hand, replace that model of synthesis with what they call a "double articulation": first, the raw materials that will make up a new entity must be selected and pre-processed; second, they must be consolidated into a whole with properties of its own. A rock like limestone or sandstone, for example, is first articulated though a process of sedimentation (the slow gathering and sorting of the pebbles that are the component parts of the rock). Then it is articulated a second time as the accumulated sediment is glued together by a process of cementation. They use Hjemslev's terms "content" and "expression" as the names for the two articulations, but this is not meant to suggest that the articulations are in any way linguistic in origin. On the contrary: the sounds, words, and grammatical patterns of a language are materials that accumulate or sediment historically, then they are consolidated by another process, like the standardization of a dialect by a Royal Academy and its official dictionaries, grammars, and rules of pronunciation.

The question of the "individuation of trajectories" is about mathematical models (which to me are the secret of the success of science) but you are correct that it goes beyond that. All entities synthesized historically are individual entities: individual plants and animals; individual species and ecosystems; individual mountains, planets, solar systems, et cetera. Here "individual" means simply "singular or unique," that is, not a particular member of a general category, but a unique entity that may compose larger individual entities through a relation of part-to-whole, like individual pebbles composing a larger individual rock. A materialist ontology of individual entities is implicit in Deleuze & Guattari and Braudel, so we must give them credit for that, then move on and invent the rest.

Q2: Neo-materialism is in a way rewriting academia as a whole, which includes the disciplinary boundaries that organize it today. In your work you definitely practice this by reading a geology into sociology for instance. Yet it would be very interesting to make this more explicit. Thus, how would new materialism propose a rethinking of the disciplinary boundaries (without using labels such as interdisciplinarity, postdisciplinarity or transdisciplinarity which eventually are all new disciplining exercises)?

MD: Academic fields are also historical individuals with contingent boundaries, many of which are settled as part of turf wars. Why would anyone feel the need to respect those boundaries? We need to draw on the conceptual and empirical resources developed by all fields to enrich materialism and prevent it from becoming *a priori*. What label we use to designate this maneuver is entirely irrelevant.

Q3: Despite your emphasis on individuated trajectories, you responded very positively to our request for an interview about a new materialism. You said that the time has come indeed for a renewed interest in materialist perspectives. In addition to its potential disciplining effects ("new materialism" becoming a theoretical yet anti-methodological school), we all know that materialism, in European thought, has a strong Marxist history. In several of your writings and interviews, however, you mentioned various problems with Marx's thinking. You consider yourself to be left-wing, but you do not share many of the dogmas, institutional preferences and economic solutions offered by the Left, premised on Marxism. In terms of economics your interest seems to be much more in institutional or evolutionary economics (think of the writings of Donald now Deirdre McCloskey and Phil Mirowski) and the way in which they now re-read Adam Smith (especially his Theory of Moral Sentiments *from 1759). Nevertheless, what you do take from Marx is his interest in the oppressed, that is, his anti-Aristotelianism that allows us to conceptualize the self-organizing power of "matter" without the "meaning" that should overcode it.*

Combining your rejection of Marx and your appraisal of materialism, could we then label your new materialist thinking as a non-humanist and even non-anthropocentric materialism?

MD: The political economy of Marx is entirely *a priori*. Although he was sincerely interested in historical data (and hence, in creating an *a posteriori* theory) the actual amount of information available to him was extremely limited. Today we have the opposite situation thanks to the work of Fernand Braudel and his school. In addition, the old institutional school of economics (perhaps best represented by the work of John Kenneth Galbraith) as well as the neo-institutionalist school, offer new models that go beyond classical economics. (The two authors you mention, though, are mostly useless, being meta-economists and non-materialist.) It is our duty as Leftists to cut the umbilical cord chaining us to Marx and reinvent political economy. Deleuze and Guattari failed miserably in this regard.

Marx's theory of value was indeed anthropocentric: only human labor was a source of value, not steam engines, coal, industrial organization, et cetera. So in that sense the answer is yes, we need to move beyond that and reconceptualize industrial production. In addition, Marx did not see trade or credit as sources of wealth, but Braudel presents indisputable historical evidence that they are.

Q4: It would be interesting, in reply to Marxism, to see this stance formulated into a political program. Above all, the current ecological drama might be a nice starting point for a neo-materialist political program. But could it be led by an invisible hand?

MD: Ecologists (not only activists but scientists) are well placed to help in this regard, because as they study food webs they must consider all sources of "value": the sun, the photosynthetic process that transforms solar energy into chemical energy, the micro-organisms that decompose dead bodies and re-inject nutrients into the soil, et cetera. Combining ecology and economics is a good idea, so that a barrel of oil is not valued only in terms of its market price but as a non-renewable source of value due to the energy it contains. We may keep the idea of an "invisible hand" (that is, that prices self-organize as part of a dynamic between supply and demand) but only when dealing with large numbers of small firms without market power. When dealing with oligopolies there is no anonymous competition but rivalry and deliberate planning. Large corporations, as Galbraith argued long ago, are a "planning system" operating through a very visible hand. Braudel referred to oligopolies as an "anti-market" to stress this point.

Q5: In your work on "assemblage theory" (in A New Philosophy of Society *from 2006) you once again show us that it is "the movement that in reality generates all these emergent wholes" that we should focus on when we want to "get a sense of the irreducible social complexity characterizing the contemporary world" (DeLanda 2006, 6). You argue strongly against the dualisms that have been transmitted to us in the history of philosophy (matter vs. meaning, micro vs. macro, inorganic vs. organic vs. social, realism vs. social constructivism, etcetera.) and argue in favor of a new ontology according to which "mechanisms are largely causal, but they do not necessarily involve* linear causality*" (ibid., 19; original emphasis). In an interesting book from 2007 called* Built by Animals, *Mike Hansell describes to us the following construction:*

> *It is a sphere composed of a few hundred stones cemented together, with a large circular hole at the bottom. The top of its dome bears seven or eight study spikes, each a cairn of stones, larger ones at the base, the smallest at the tip creating a sharp point. The most distinctive architectural detail, the one that gives the name to the species that builds it, is the collar to the circular aperture. It is a pleated coronet constructed from particles too small to be distinguishable from the cement that binds them. The diameter of this whole dwelling, for that is what it is, is about 150 thousandths of a millimeter (i.e. micrometres, written µm). Smaller than the full stop at the end of this sentence, it is the portable home of the* Difflugia coronata, *a species of amoeba (Hansell 2007, 58).*

The Difflugia coronata *is not an animal. It is a single-cell creature that feeds and reproduces, but has no nervous system (thus no brain). Major academics interested in animal architecture, like the quoted Hansell, have difficulty explaining how such a simple creature is capable of creating such a complex form, their biggest problem being that the* Difflugia coronata *lacks a brain. For some reason they fail to see how their question already embodies several presumptions that make any answer impossible. They accept the Cartesian difference between the mind and the body. They accept the difference between the animal (subject) and its house (object).*

New materialism, implicitly and explicitly, wards off these modernist oppositions, and might very well be considered capable of explaining how this simple creature could create such complex forms. Not only in your geological history of the organic world, but also in your assemblage theory you show us how organic and inorganic matter, in their entanglement, create the new. Do you think the Difflugia coronata *created its house similarly to the way in which the human being created not only its cities but also the social group equally "[...] freeing them from the constraints and literally setting them into motion to conquer every available niche in the air, in water and on land" as you wrote in* A Thousand Years of Nonlinear History *(2000, 26–7)?*

MD: It is absurd to think that complex self-organizing structures need a "brain" to generate them. The coupled system atmosphere-hydrosphere is continuously generating structures (thunderstorms, hurricanes, coherent wind currents) not only without a brain but without any organs whatsoever. The ancient chemistry of the prebiotic soup also generated such coherent structures (auto-catalytic loops) without which the genetic code could not have emerged. And bacteria in the first two billion years of the history of the biosphere discovered all major means to tap into energy sources (fermentation, photosynthesis, respiration). To think that a "brain" is needed goes beyond Cartesian dualism and fades into Creationism: matter is an inert receptacle for forms that come from the outside imposed by an exterior psychic agency: "Let there be light!"

So yes, neo-materialism is based on the idea that matter has morphogenetic capacities of its own and does not need to be commanded into generating form. But we should not attempt to build such a philosophy by "rejecting dualisms" or following any other meta-recipe. The idea that we know already how all past discourses have been generated, that we have the secret of all past conceptual systems, and that we can therefore engage in meta-theorizing based on that knowledge is deeply mistaken. And this mistake is at the source of all the idealisms that have been generated by postmodernism.

Q6: Could you elaborate some more on this idea of not "rejecting dualisms," since this comes very close to an important argument in our own reading of new materialism. For when we say that new materialism, implicitly and explicitly, wards off modernist oppositions and thus qualitatively shifts the acceptance of the Cartesian difference between the mind and the body, the subject and the object, et cetera, we are referring to Bergson ([1869] 2004, 297) who has argued that: "The difficulties of ordinary dualism come, not from the distinction of the two terms, but from the impossibility of seeing how the one is grafted upon the other." Thus, we argue, the time has come to make a formal difference between this ordinary dualism as Bergson analyzes it, and the radical rewriting of modernist dualisms, as proposed for instance by Lyotard and Deleuze. The latter have set themselves to a rewriting exercise that involves a movement in thought that practices what Bergson termed "pushing dualism to an extreme," rephrased by Deleuze's statement that "difference is pushed to the limit." Would you agree with us that this is actually a crucial element of new materialism's affirmative stance?

MD: I am not convinced that avoiding dualities is the key to a new way of thinking (particularly if one simply adds new ones: modernism-postmodernism, rhizome-tree, power-resistance). What matters is what categories are used dualistically. For example, in my book *A New Philosophy of Society: Assemblage Theory and Social Complexity* (DeLanda 2006) I criticize the use of the concepts "The Market" and "The State." Not because they are a duality, but because both are reified generalities that do not really exist. Adding a third term, like "The People," would not help. What we need is to replace the reified generalities with concrete assemblages: many bazaars, many regional trading areas, many national markets… each with a date of birth and (potentially) a date of death. The best way to deal with this problem is always to think statistically, dealing always with populations and with how variation is distributed in a population. Thus, the duality "male-female" can easily be eliminated if we take a large population and check how secondary sexual characteristics are distributed: all of them, except for the capacity to bear children, form two overlapping statistical distributions. The duality emerges when one ignores the zone of overlap and reifies the averages.

Q7: Could we say that this stance exemplifies your ontological take on 'topology' as explained in Intensive Science and Virtual Philosophy, *which involves a qualitative shifting of Euclidean geometry (2002, 24) through "view[ing] this genesis not as an abstract mathematical process but as a concrete physical process in which an undifferentiated intensive space (that is, a space defined by continuous intensive properties) progressively differentiates, eventually giving rise to extensive structures (discontinuous structures with definite metric properties)" (ibid., 25; original emphasis)?*

MD: Topology enters neo-materialism as part of the rejection of Aristotle. We need to replace both his "genus" and his "species." The latter is replaced by the concept of a species as a contingent historical individual, born through a process of speciation (reproductive isolation) and capable of dying through extinction. The former is replaced by the "topological animal," that is, a body-plan common to entire phyla (such as that of vertebrates) that is a structured space of possible body designs. Such a space cannot be metric because each vertebrate species varies in length, area, volume, et cetera, so only topological properties like connectivity can be used to specify it.

Q8: In After Finitude, *Quentin Meillassoux critiques idealists and what he calls "correlationists," for their shared representationalism (something you also argue against) and also for continuing the anthropocentrism that saturates the history of Western thought. For although the human mind is no longer the point of departure for philosophy, correlationism still needs it in order for the world to exist. Meillassoux ([2006] 2008, 37) ascribes a Kantianism to "the Leibnizian monad; Schelling's nature, or the objective subject-object; Hegelian Mind; Schopenhauer's Will; the Will (or* Wills*) to Power in Nietzsche; perception loaded with memory in Bergson; Deleuze's Life, etc."*

According to our reading of your work, you seem to aim at providing a non-anthropocentric mapping of the morphogenetic changes of the real. Does it follow from this summary of your project that you agree with Meillassoux?

MD: To be honest, I never read Meillassoux. But I surely reject the idea that morphogenesis needs any "mind" to operate. I also reject the neo-

Kantian thesis of the linguisticality of experience. To assume that human experience is structured conceptually is to dehistoricize the human species: we spent hundreds of thousands of years as a social species, with a division of labor (hunters, gatherers) and sophisticated stone tool technology. Language is a relatively recent acquisition. Are we to assume that those ancient hunter gatherers lived in an amorphous world waiting for language to give it form? That's Creationism again, you know: "And the word became flesh."

So yes, to the extent that Meillassoux rejects all forms of idealism I surely agree with him. I would need to see what he offers beyond a critique in order to assess the actual degree of agreement. Critique is never enough. Marxism is not going to go away simply by making a critique of it, we need to offer a viable alternative.

Q9: If so, an alliance can also be struck between your work and the work of Alain Badiou, who is Meillassoux's teacher and also claiming a new materialism. This time it comes to the fore when we take into account your shared interest in mathematics, and, more in particular, topology, diagram or model. For a new materialism to be valuable for scholarly and activist projects such as feminism and post-colonialism, however, a theory of the subject seems to be necessary. In new feminist materialism, for instance, alliances are sought with process ontologies, which make the non-anthropocentric stance not *non-foundationalist (cf. the work of Rosi Braidotti). A question then would be whether you see this necessity for a new theory of the subject, and how this (dis-)connects with the work of Meillassoux and Badiou?*

MD: Badiou left me with a bad feeling after reading his book on Deleuze which is incredibly incompetent. He uses the word "the One" on just about every page when Deleuze never used it (other than when making remarks about the scholastic notion of the "univocity of being"). He is also a fanatic about set theory, whereas I tend towards the differential calculus as my mathematical base. (The idea that the latter was reduced to the former is yet another mistake we inherited from the nineteenth century).

I agree that a theory of the subject is absolutely necessary but it must be based on Hume, not on Kant: subjective experience not as organized conceptually by categories but as literally composed of intensities (of color, sound, aroma, flavor, texture) that are given structure by habitual action.

Recent developments in artificial intelligence will help with this: while the old symbolic school is deeply Kantian, the new connectionist school (based on neural nets that are not programmed but trained) points to a way out. Current neural net designs are at the level of insect intelligence but they already suggest how an insect protosubjectivity can emerge from a dynamic of perceived intensities. We need to extend this to the subjectivity of mammals and birds, and work our way up to human subjectivity. The political implication of this can be phrased as follows: rejecting the linguisticality of experience (according to which every culture lives in its own world) leads to a conception of a shared human experience in which the variation comes not from differences in signification (which is a linguistic notion), but of significance (which is a pragmatic one). Different cultures do attribute different importance, relevance, or significance to different things because their practices (not their minds) are different. When it comes to gender, the paradox is this: idealism was created by males who were in an academic environment in which their material practices were reduced to a minimum, and who had wives who did all the material work. And yet the moment feminism became academic it became deeply idealist. Hence I welcome any return to materialism by feminists, even if based on entirely different ideas.

Chapter 3
"Matter feels, converses, suffers, desires, yearns and remembers"
Interview with Karen Barad

Q1: "New materialism" as a term was coined by Manuel DeLanda and Rosi Braidotti in the second half of the 1990's[1]. New materialism shows how the mind is always already material (the mind is an idea of the body), how matter is necessarily something of the mind (the mind has the body as its object), and how nature and culture are always already "naturecultures" (Donna Haraway's term). New materialism opposes the transcendental and humanist (dualist) traditions that are haunting cultural theory, standing on the brink of both the modern and the post-postmodern era. The transcendental and humanist traditions, which are manifold yet consistently predicated on dualist structures, continue to stir debates that are being opened up by new materialists (think of the feminist polemic concerning the failed materialism in the work of Judith Butler, and of the Saussurian/Lacanian linguistic heritage in media and cultural studies). What can be labelled "new materialism" shifts these dualist structures by allowing for the conceptualization of the travelling of the fluxes of nature and culture, matter and mind, and opening up active theory formation.

In your emphasis on quantum physics, you seem to be proposing a very similar route. The idea behind "agential realism," in print since 1996 following the Bohrian approach to epistemology that you have published about since the mid-1980s, seems to ward off the dualisms that have haunted the humanities and the sciences as well. Particularly in the case of measurement, this agential realism allows you to re-read Bohr's philosophy of quantum mechanics and to critique the fact that so many theorists refuse to come to terms with the material-discursive and performative nature of intra-actions.

Is this immanent enfolding of matter and meaning, which you refer to as "agential realism," and which we name a "new materialism," the quintessence of your critique of both the sciences and the humanities?

Karen Barad: The core of your question I have to say is spot on, but since you state what I am doing in terms of critique I wanted to start by saying something about critique. I am not interested in critique. In my opinion, critique is over-rated, over-emphasized, and over-utilized, to the detriment of feminism. As Bruno Latour signals in an article entitled "Why has critique run out of steam? From Matters of Fact to Matters of Concern" (2004), critique is a tool that keeps getting used out of habit perhaps, but it is no longer the tool needed for the kinds of situations we now face. Critique has been the tool of choice for so long, and our students find themselves so well-trained in critique that they can spit out a critique with the push of a button. Critique is too easy, especially when a commitment to reading with care no longer seems to be a fundamental element of critique. So as I explain to my students, reading and writing are ethical practices, and critique misses the mark. Now, I understand that there is a different valence to the notion of critique in Europe than there is in the United States; nonetheless, I think this point is important. Critique is all too often not a deconstructive practice, that is, a practice of reading for the constitutive exclusions of those ideas we can not do without, but a destructive practice meant to dismiss, to turn aside, to put someone or something down— another scholar, another feminist, a discipline, an approach, et cetera. So this is a practice of negativity that I think is about subtraction, distancing and othering. Latour suggests that we might turn to Alan Turing's notion of the critical instead of critique (Turing 1950), where going critical refers to the notion of critical mass—that is, when a single neutron enters a critical sample of nuclear material which produces a branching chain reaction that explodes with ideas. As a physicist I find this metaphor chilling and ominous. Instead, building on a suggestion of Donna Haraway, what I propose is the practice of diffraction, of reading diffractively for patterns of differences that make a difference. And I mean that not as an additive notion opposed to subtraction, as I will explain in a little bit. Rather, I mean that in the sense of it being suggestive, creative and visionary.

In chapter 2 of *Meeting the Universe Halfway: Quantum Physics and the Entanglement of Matter and Meaning* (Barad 2007) I discussed in detail what I call a diffractive methodology, a method of diffractively reading insights through one another, building new insights, and attentively and carefully reading for differences that matter in their fine details, together with the recognition that there intrinsic to this analysis is an ethics that is not predicated on externality but rather entanglement. Diffractive readings bring inventive provocations; they are good to think with. They are respectful, detailed, ethical engagements. I want to come back to the crux of your question now that I have said something about critique. I do not mean to pick on that, but I think it is important to say something about the notion of critique and to move it to thinking instead about these kinds of provocations and other kinds of engagements that we might practice.

So, coming back to the crux of your question, the entanglement of matter and meaning calls into question this set of dualisms that places nature on one side and culture on the other. And which separates off matters of fact from matters of concern (Bruno Latour) and matters of care (Maria Puig de la Bellacasa), and shifts them off to be dealt with by what we aptly call here in the States "separate academic divisions," whereby the division of labor is such that the natural sciences are assigned matters of fact and the humanities matters of concern, for example. It is difficult to see the diffraction patterns—the patterns of difference that make a difference—when the cordoning off of concerns into separate domains elides the resonances and dissonances that make up diffraction patterns that make the entanglements visible.

I would like to offer two examples to think with in engaging your question. I recently gave a keynote at a conference at the Stevens Institute of Technology,[2] which is in New Jersey. They are starting a very innovative revamping of their Humanities program. They are interested in taking insights from science studies, and running them back into the Humanities. This is the way they talk about it. What they propose is the reverse of how some would think of the potential impact of science studies: not to use the Humanities to think about the Sciences but to use the Sciences to rethink the Humanities. This is their project and it was a very interesting conference. But there was something about the way in which it was being framed overall that I wanted to see if I could get into conversation with them about. First of all, there was the notion that what is needed is a synthesis; a synthesis or a joining of the Humanities and the Sciences as if they were always already separate rather than always already entangled. So that there would be Science with matters of fact, and nature, and so on, on one side, and Humanities, meaning, values, and culture, on the other, and somehow that there would be a joining of the two. So, we talked about the ways in which there are entanglements that already exist between the Humanities and the Sciences; they have not grown up separately from one another. I was just pointing out to them some of the limitations of thinking analogically as in looking for mirror images between the Sciences on the one hand and the Humanities on the other. And I was telling them about this wonderful story that Sharon Traweek tells about when she was doing fieldwork on the high energy physics community at the Stanford Linear Accelerator (SLAC). She is standing in a hall at SLAC, and notices a physicist staring at pictures of fractal images on the wall. She gazes upon the images and asks him: "Can you tell me what is so beautiful about those images?" The physicist turns to her with this puzzled look on his face and says: "I am not really sure why you asked the question. It's self-evident! Everywhere you look it is the same." And of course feminists are not trained to look or take pleasure in everything being the same, but to think about differences.

Of course the mirror image of that is that Science mirrors Culture, so we have a kind of scientific realism versus social constructivism, which are of course both about mirroring. Instead, what I propose is the notion of diffraction, drawing on the work of my colleague and friend Donna Haraway. As Donna says, "diffraction patterns record the history of interaction, interference, reinforcement, difference. Diffraction is about heterogeneous history, not about originals. Unlike reflections, diffractions do not displace the same elsewhere, in more or less distorted form, thereby giving rise to industries of [story-making about origins and truths]. Rather, diffraction can be a metaphor for another kind of critical consciousness." What I was pointing out is the difference in the shift from geometrical optics, from questions of mirroring and sameness, reflexivity, where to see your image in the mirror there necessarily has to be a distance between you and the mirror. So there is a separation of subject and object, and objectivity is about mirror images of the world. And instead, the shift towards diffraction, towards differences that matter, is really a matter of what physicists call physical optics as compared to geometrical optics. Geometrical optics does not pay any attention to the nature of light. Actually, it is an approximation that gets used to study the optics of different lenses, or mirrors. And you just treat light as if it were a ray (an abstract notion). In other words, it is completely agnostic about whether light is a particle or a wave or anything else. It is just an approximation scheme for studying various apparatuses. By contrast, diffraction allows you to study both the nature of the apparatus and also the object. That is, both the nature of light and also the nature of the apparatus itself. I talk a lot about this in chapter 2 of *Meeting*. But what I wanted to bring out is the fact that we learn so much more about diffraction using quantum physics.

There is a difference between understanding diffraction as a classical physics phenomenon and understanding it quantum-mechanically. I have taken this wonderful metaphor that Donna has given us and I have run with it by adding important non-classical insights from quantum physics. Diffraction, understood using quantum physics, is not just a matter of interference, but of entanglement, an ethico-onto-epistemological matter. This difference is very important. It underlines the fact that knowing is a direct material engagement, a cutting together-apart, where cuts do violence but also open up and rework the agential conditions of possibility. There is not this knowing from a distance. Instead of there being a separation of subject and object, there is an entanglement of subject and object, which is called the "phenomenon." Objectivity, instead of being about offering an undistorted mirror image of the world, is about accountability to marks on bodies, and responsibility to the entanglements of which we are a part. That is the kind of shift that we get, if we move diffraction into the realm of quantum physics. All of this is to say that we come up with a different way of thinking about what insights the Sciences, the Humanities, the Arts, the Social Sciences, and let's not forget insights derived outside of academia, can bring to one another by diffractively reading them through one another for their various entanglements, and by being attentive to what gets excluded as well as what comes to matter. So that we wind up with a very different way of engaging the relationship between the Sciences and the Humanities, which I think is the original question that you asked me.

And then, just really briefly my second example and I promise you I will not go on this long about every question, but just to set up some things in the beginning... I taught a lecture course this quarter called "Feminism in Science," which had Science students in the class as well as students from the Humanities, the Social Sciences, and the Arts, and we were talking about the notion of scientific literacy and how scientific literacy has grown up to be the sole responsibility of the Sciences. But what is scientific literacy? We spent millions of dollars on it in the United States and we are not really sure what it means at all, as a matter of fact. And after spending millions of dollars by whatever measure is provided for scientific literacy, we still have the same percentages of scientific literacy as before. According to these measures, scientific literacy is between three and six percent. And that is actually the same number of scientists and engineers that we have. That tells you something about the way in which scientific literacy is being understood, and how it is being measured, and how it is being thought about, and who needs to take responsibility for it, and so on. And so we talked about the fact that a different kind of literacy is actually required for doing science. That consideration of the ethical, social and legal implications of various new sciences and technologies after the fact is not robust enough. For example, we considered the new field of bioethics in which ethics is taken to be solely a matter of considering the imagined consequences of scientific projects that are already given. But the notion of consequences is based on the wrong temporality: asking after potential consequences is too little, too late, because ethics of course, is being done right at the lab bench. And so, as for what it takes to be scientifically literate, the question is what does it take in order to identify the various apparatuses of bodily production that are at stake here. And so in order to identify those we need a much broader sense of literacy and we need all kinds of people around the lab bench, so that scientific literacy should no longer be seen as being solely the responsibility of the Sciences. I think that is one of the ways in which we get ourselves in a lot of trouble in terms of education.

Q2: Could you explain to us a bit more what, how, or who the agent in agential realism "is"?

KB: First, I want to say that I try to stay away from using the term "agent," or even "actant," because these terms work against the relational ontology I am proposing. Also the notion that there are agents who have agency, or who grant agency, say, to non-humans (the granting of agency is an ironic notion, no?), pulls us back into the same old humanist orbits over and over again. And it is not easy to resist the gravitational force of humanism, especially when it comes to the question of "agency." But agency for me is not something that someone or something *has* to varying degrees, since I am trying to displace the very notion of independently existing individuals. This is not, however, to deny agency in its importance, but on the contrary, to rework the notion of agency in ways that are appropriate to relational ontologies. Agency is not held, it is not a property of persons or things; rather, agency is an enactment, a matter of possibilities for reconfiguring entanglements. So agency is not about choice in any liberal humanist sense; rather, it is about the possibilities and accountability entailed in reconfiguring material-discursive apparatuses of bodily production, including the boundary articulations and exclusions that are marked by those practices. One of the items that you asked about is the *how* of agency, and in a sense, the *how* is precisely in the specificity of the particular practices, so I cannot give a general answer to that, but perhaps I can say something helpful about the space of possibilities for agency.

Agency, on an agential realist account, does not require a clash of apparatuses, (as Butler once suggested) such as the contradictory norms of femininity, so that we are never successful in completely embodying femininity, because there are contradictory requirements. Agential realism does not require that kind of clash of apparatuses, because intra-actions to begin with are never determining, even when apparatuses are reinforcing. Intra-actions entail exclusions, and exclusions foreclose determinism. However, once determinism is foreclosed this does not leave us with the option of free will. I think we tend to think about causality and questions of agency in terms of either determinism on the one hand, or free will on the other. Cause and effect are supposed to follow one upon the other like billiard balls, and so we got into the habit of saying that we do not really mean this in a causal sense. And I think to some degree, causality has become a dirty word, as realism is/was. And so I am trying to get people to talk about causality again, because I think that it is very, very important. If we have a group of people where we find that there is a lot of cancer in a certain community, I want to know something about the nature of that community and about causal relationships, because if I am at Love Canal in the United States, a populated area where a bunch of toxins were dumped and the people were getting cancers, then I might want to evacuate people. On the other hand, if I am at the Mayo Clinic, where they are treating cancer patients and there are a lot of people with cancer, it is not the thing to do. I really want us to specify more carefully the different kinds of causalities, and how to think causality again. And that is partly what I mean by the notion of "intra-action" as proposing a new way of thinking causality. It is not just a kind of neologism, which gets us to shift from interaction, where we start with separate entities and they interact, to intra-action, where there are interactions through which subject and object emerge, but actually as a new understanding of causality itself.

First of all, agency is about response-ability, about the possibilities of mutual response, which is not to deny, but to attend to power imbalances. Agency is about possibilities for worldly re-configurings. So agency is not something possessed by humans, or non-humans for that matter. It is an enactment. And it enlists, if you will, "non-humans" as well as "humans." At the same time, I want to be clear that what I am *not* talking about here is democratically distributing agency across an assemblage of humans and non-humans. Even though there are no agents per se, the notion of agency I am suggesting does not go against the crucial point of power imbalances. On the contrary. The specificity of intra-actions speaks to the particularities of the power imbalances of the complexity of a field of forces. I know that some people are very nervous about not having agency localized in the human subject, but I think that is the first step—recognizing that there is not this kind of localization or particular characterization of the human subject is the first step in taking account of power imbalances, not an undoing of it.

As a brief example, there is an article I just came across on the Internet by Chris Wilbert called "Profit, Plague and Poultry: The Intra-active Worlds of Highly Pathogenic Avian Flu" (Wilbert 2006), on the bio-geopolitics of potential flu pandemics. Chris's analysis of the avian flu (H5N1) as a naturalcultural phenomenon highlights the importance of taking account of the agential entanglements of intra-acting human and non-human practices. Chris points out that while world health organizations and governments are placing migratory birds and small farm chicken producers under surveillance, the empirical data does not support these causal linkages. Rather, the disease follows the geographical diffraction patterns of large-scale factory farmed production of poultry. The latter gives rise to unprecedented densities of birds, making first-class lodgings for thriving and mutating zoonoses. Industrially produced meats, international veterinary practices, biosecurity practices, international trade agreements, transport networks, increased density of human populations, and more are among the various agential apparatuses at work. Causality is not interactional, but rather intra-actional. Making policy based on additive approaches to multiple causes, misses key factors in avoiding epidemics such as providing inexpensive forms of safe food for the poorest populations and the elimination of industrial forms of the mass killing of animals. So in addition to nicely illustrating the importance of paying attention to "human" and "non-human" forms of agency, as it were, there is a way in which Chris acknowledges what gets left out of practices of accounting when agency is attributed to human or non-human entities and left at that. What gets left out, you see, is a whole array of very complex material practices that contribute to a kind of epidemic that is not attributable either to the organisms themselves or to the kinds of things that people do. I do not know Chris. I bring it to your attention, because I think that he gives us an interesting case to think with.

Another example that may be helpful here is an example that Haraway (2008) talks about. It is an example that is raised by Barbara Smuts, who is an American bioanthropologist who went to Tanzania to investigate baboons in the wild for her doctoral research. She is told as a scientific investigator of non-human primates to keep her distance, so that her presence would not influence the behavior of the research subjects that she was studying. Distance is the condition of objectivity. Smuts talks about the fact that this advice was a complete disaster for her research, that she found herself unable to do any observations since the baboons were constantly attentive to what she was doing. She finally realized that this was because Smuts was behaving so strangely to them, they just could not get over her. She was being a bad social subject in their circles. The only way to carry on and to do research objectively was to be responsible; that is, that objectivity, a theme that feminist science studies has been emphasizing all along, is the fact that objectivity is a matter of responsibility and not a matter of distancing at all. What ultimately did work was that she learned to be completely responsive to the non-human primates, and in that way she became a good baboon citizen. They could understand, at least intelligibly to the non-human primates, and as a result they left her alone and went about their business, making it possible for her to conduct her research.

Q3: *In* Meeting the Universe Halfway *and in several journal articles, you follow Haraway in proposing "diffraction," the relational nature of difference, as a methodology for treating theories and texts not as preexisting entities, but as intra-action, as forces from which other texts come into existence. On the other hand, you focus strongly on the work of Niels Bohr throughout your work. Your rewriting of the philosophy that is active in all of his texts seems to be neither dutiful nor undutiful to his ideas. And yet your work can be read as one of the strongest commentaries on the work of Bohr now available to academics. Perhaps the first one that succeeds in reading him into the Humanities. Next to Bohr, of course, you read many other scientists and scholars like Einstein, Schrödinger, but also Merleau-Ponty, Haraway of course, Deleuze, and Latour. Especially as concerns the philosophers and those scholars traditionally not read within the Sciences, you seem to read them very affirmatively, albeit in passing.*

How would you evaluate this conceptualization of the way in which you treat theories, taking into account your proposal for a diffractive methodology? In other words, is there a sense in which your work is not a meditation that agrees or disagrees with the work of Bohr, but one that is intra-active with it, creating both the work of Bohr and agential realism? And what are the generational implications of diffraction more generally? Feminists are usually wary of thought as governed by oedipality; feminists such as Rosi Braidotti have argued for a methodology that does not repeat the all-too-common Oedipal relation with Masters, affirming their status by negating the work, and this comes very close to your critique of critique actually. Does diffraction allow for a relation between texts and scholars that is neither undutiful (affirming the Master by negating the work) nor dutiful (placing the "new" work in the Master's house)?

KB: Given what I already said about diffractive readings, I think it is clear that your question really beautifully states my relationship with the materials that I engaged with in doing diffractive readings. In the spirit of diffractive readings, I just want to say that I am really very grateful and indebted to you for your careful reading of my work. Thank you for that. I wholeheartedly agree with what you have said there in terms of the fact that I am neither looking to Bohr's work as scripture nor to somehow be the "undutiful daughter" to Bohr. But to read various insights through one another and to produce something new, new patterns of thinking-being, while at the same time being very attentive to what it is that Bohr is trying to say to us, and I think that you have done that with my work so I wanted to thank you for that.

Q4: Although "gender" is the term that seems to be the unquestionable foundation of the field of gender studies, its conceptual legacy has been specified as Anglo-American and linguistic. Feminist scholars working with gender usually set up an argument against a biological determinism or biological essentialism, and ascribe a fixed sexual ontology to major traditions in (scholarly) thought as well as to Continental feminist philosophy (e.g. the work of Luce Irigaray). Félix Guattari once summarized his take on these issues in an interview, stating:

> *If Gilles Deleuze and I have adopted the position of practically not speaking of sexuality, and instead speaking of desire, it's because we consider that the problems of life and creation are never reducible to physiological functions, reproductive functions, to some particular dimension of the body. They always involve elements that are either beyond the individual in the social or political field, or else before the individual level (Guattari and Rolnik [1982] 2008, 411).*

This non-representationalist take on "sexual difference" seems to come close to your reading of this concept. Your proposal for an onto-epistemology shows us how matter (among others bodily matter) and meaning are always already immanently enfolded and transitional. Yet instead of taking a term from psychoanalysis (like desire), you bring in physics (Bohr's conceptual apparatus). How then is quantum physics helping you in articulating your feminism?

KB: A decade ago I would often get the following question: "Since your work is not about women or gender, what does it have to do with feminism?" My answer, of course, was: "Everything." Happily, the question you have asked is light years beyond the kind of thinking that motivates that question. And I am assuming then that the level of conversation has shifted since that time, and that I can jump right in. Eros, desire, life forces run through everything, not only specific body parts or specific kind of engagements among body parts. Matter itself is not a substrate or a medium for the flow of desire. Materiality itself is always already a desiring dynamism, a reiterative reconfiguring, energized and energizing, enlivened and enlivening. I have been particularly interested in how matter comes to matter. How matter makes itself felt. This is a feminist project whether or not there are any women or people or any other macroscopic beings in sight. Along with other new materialist feminists—Vicki Kirby is notable in this regard—feeling, desiring and experiencing are not singular characteristics or capacities of human consciousness. Matter feels, converses, suffers, desires, yearns and remembers. You could also see Noela Davis' paper on new materialism on this topic (Davis 2009). I tried to make this point more vivid in chapter 7 of my book, which has received a lot of interest and attention, but less specifically feminist engagement. And I think there is a lot of important food for thought in this chapter, at least in my mind. So I want to go over this, because it is a chapter that gets deeply into the physics of things, and as a result many humanities and social sciences scholars assume it is irrelevant to what they are thinking about. I always teach physics in my feminist classes, in part precisely because it calls into question the exceptionally narrow framing of scientific concerns and scientific literacy in the way that I was just talking about. Who is responsible for engaging with science? I'd like to walk you through some of what's going on in that chapter, because I think it holds some really important ways for rethinking some key feminist issues about matter and space and time and so on.

I will give you a super-fast lesson of what you need to know about quantum physics and then come to what is in Chapter 7 to show you some of the results and what I think the implications are in terms of thinking about questions of social justice, which I think are key here. So here is my crash course on quantum physics.

According to classical physics, there are only two kinds of entities in the world; there are particles and there are waves. Particles are very different from waves. Particles are localized entities that occupy a particular place in space and in time, and you cannot have two particles in the same place at the same time. On the other hand, there are waves, and waves are not entities at all. Waves are disturbances in fields. If you think about ocean waves, you see that waves often overlap with one another. They *can* occupy the same place at the same time; that is part of what they are famous for doing. So on the one hand, we have something localized, and, on the other, we have something very non-localized. Very distinct kinds of entities, ontologically speaking. In physics, there is a very simple machine that can be used to find out whether it is a particle or a wave, and it is called a two-slit apparatus. When you take a bunch of balls and shoot them randomly at two slits, what you find is that most of the particles wind up directly across from the two slits. You get something called a "scatter pattern." You can think about the fact that if I am wildly throwing tennis balls in this room at the doorway, most of them are going to wind up right across from the doorway and a few of them will scatter to the sides. In contrast to that, think of a wave machine, making a disturbance in the water. And when the disturbance hits this kind of "breakwater" with two holes in it, what happens is that the disturbance bulges out on both sides and you get these kinds of concentric, overlapping circles that get forced through, just like when I drop two rocks in a pond simultaneously, I get an overlapping of concentric circles. That is a diffraction pattern and what you see is that there is a reinforcing of waves. When two waves meet, crest to crest, they make a higher wave. But sometimes you get a crest meeting a trough, and they cancel out. That makes for a very different kind of pattern.

Now, what happens if we test electrons with a two-slit apparatus? You might think, since we used to think of electrons as little tiny particles, that they would give me a particle pattern. But the result that we actually get is that electrons exhibit a diffraction or wave pattern. But as we saw, diffraction patterns are created by overlapping waves. But how can electrons overlap? They are particles. They cannot overlap with one another. You might think that the electrons are overlapping, but you can test that by sending one electron through at a time. If you send just one electron through at a time, you built up this diffraction pattern. It seems like we cannot explain this diffraction pattern; it seems like a mystery how this particle seems to be acting like a wave. Einstein in particular was very upset about this and suggested that we do an experiment where we actually watch the electron go through the slits. I want to talk about this which-slit detector experiment, because this is what I am building up to. In this experiment, what I have done is replace the top slit with a slit on a spring. And if the particle goes through the top slit, it imparts some of its momentum to the top slit and it moves a little bit, then I will know "Oh, it went through the top slit." So, this is a way to measure which slit the electron is going through on its way to the screen. And Einstein said if we do this experiment we will catch the electron in the act of being both a particle, by going through one slit or the other, and a wave by showing this interference pattern and then it will show that quantum mechanics is self-contradictory and that we will have to find some other way of thinking about it. And Bohr said: "No, not so fast." If you do this experiment, you have now revised the apparatus. And what we observe in any experiment is a *phenomenon* or entanglement or the inseparability of the apparatus and the observed object. Bohr said that if Einstein were to make the adjustment to the two-slit apparatus he suggested, he is going to get a particle pattern, not a diffraction pattern. Now, one should lose sleep over this. Because what this is saying is that the ontology of the electron is changing depending upon how I measure it. Let me just finish the quantum physics lesson really quickly. Bohr has an explanation for this, which is to say, again, that the properties that we measure are not attributable to independent objects. Independent objects are abstract notions. This is the wrong objective referent. The actual objective referent is the phenomenon—the intra-action of what we call the electron and the apparatus. And so the fact that its ontology changes when we change the apparatus is not a surprise, because we are investigating an entirely different phenomenon.

I will now move into what is in Chapter 7 because I think, again, that there are important feminist "lessons" here. And of course when I say "feminist lessons," that is a distorting shorthand I need to qualify. Because, of course, what I am presenting with agential realism already has feminist lessons built in to it, and that is part of the beauty of Chapter 7. At least for me it is the incredible satisfaction of taking insights from feminist theory, on the one hand, and insights from physics, on the other, and reading them through one another in building agential realism. And from there going back and seeing if agential realism can solve certain kinds of fundamental problems in quantum physics. And the fact that it is robust enough to do that, and that feminist theory has important things to say to physics is amazing, absolutely amazing, and key to the point I want to make as well. And in fact, when I was able to actually show that you could do science with agential realism and bring these important interests, the question came to me of whether or not I should publish this result in a physics journal or leave it for the book, so that physicists would have to go to a feminist book in order to find out some of the physics. I chose the latter, but in retrospect I think it was a mistake, because it took a very long time for the book to come out (more than three years) and because it seems that some physicists are engaging with my ideas without acknowledging it. Practices of publishing are always political.

Coming back to the issue at hand, Bohr and Heisenberg were totally at odds. Not only Bohr and Einstein, but also Bohr and Heisenberg. Heisenberg thought that the reason why it changes from a wave pattern to a particle pattern when you change the apparatus is because you are disturbing the particle. And this places a limit on what we can know, because each measurement disturbs what you are measuring. And he called that the "(Heisenberg) Uncertainty Principle," which I have found is more familiar to European audiences than American audiences. But Bohr argues with Heisenberg and says that he makes a fundamental error in proposing uncertainty, and what is at issue is not uncertainty at all, but rather indeterminacy. That is, when we make a measurement, what happens is that it is not a matter of disturbing something and our knowledge is uncertain as a result, but rather there are not inherent properties and there are not inherent boundaries of things that we want to call entities before the measurement intra-action. That is, Bohr is saying that things are indeterminate; there are no things before the measurement, and that the very act of measurement produces determinate boundaries and properties of things. So, his is an ontological principle rather than an epistemological one. In other words, for Bohr particles do not have a position independently of my measuring something called position.

Now, it seems that there is no scientific way to discern who is right, because what we are talking about is showing an empirical result about what happens before you do any measurement. So it seems like there is no way to ever resolve that. But actually we can. This is amazing! We can do experimental metaphysics now, which of course is just an indicator of the fact that there has never been a sharp boundary between physics, on the one hand, and metaphysics or philosophy, on the other. So there is an amazing and really astonishing experiment that physicists have only been able to do in the past decade or so since previously it was not technologically possible. And these famous *Gedanken-* or thought experiments of Bohr and Heisenberg could now be done for the first time, actually be performed in a laboratory. They never thought about them actually being done; they were not meant to be experiments that got actualized. They were meant to be experiments to think with, just tools to think with. But now it is technologically possible to actually do this experiment—to show what happens when I measure which-slit. Was Einstein right and do I catch the electron being both a particle and a wave showing that quantum theory is self-contradictory? Or is Bohr right that once I actually go ahead and measure which-slit, now I get a particle pattern and the interference pattern is gone? But even more beautifully than that, what the physicists have done in this case is to design an experiment where Heisenberg's explanation of disturbing something that already exists, cannot be part of the explanation. So Heisenberg is designed *out* of this experiment. If it happens, it is happening for some reason other than a disturbance.

What is happening is that there is a beam of atoms coming along; in fact, they are rubidium atoms, and before the rubidium atoms reach the double slit, what happens is that there is a laser beam which gives the rubidium atoms some energy. And what happens when the atom gets energy, the electron that is in the inner orbital of rubidium gets kicked up to a high energy level from the energy it got from the laser beam. Now it is in, what is called, an "excited state." See, there is already talk of desire in physics! And then it goes across and it goes to these cavities, these micromaser cavities. That is the which-slit detector. You do not have to know anything about micromaser cavities at all except this: when the rubidium atom in an excited state goes into one micromaser cavity or the other, the electron necessarily drops back down to its ground state and in doing so it emits a photon and it leaves this trace photon in either the upper cavity or the lower cavity and then goes on its way through the two slits. So the rubidium atom goes on its way through the two slits and it hits the screen. And that is our experiment. Now, the reason why Heisenberg is not a part of this, is because you can show that by getting the rubidium atom into an excited state and having it come back down, it does nothing to affect the atom's forward momentum. It is *not* disturbed. Here physicists have very cleverly made a which-slit detector that does not disturb the rubidium atoms' forward momentum. So it is going to leave a telltale trace in detector one or detector two of which slit it went through without disturbing it. Now if you do this without the which-slit detector, just send rubidium atoms through double slits, you get a diffraction pattern. But if you put the laser there and the micromaser cavities and find out which slit it goes through, then it shifts to a scatter pattern or a particle pattern. But that second one definitely is a scatter pattern (rather than the alternating intensity pattern of waves). I just told you that there is no disturbance going on here so that is amazing already. It is amazing that you can now show that Bohr is right and not Einstein.

But now here is where we as feminists really need to pay attention, because now something really amazing is coming forward in this, which is that since I have not made a disturbance in actually measuring which slit the atom goes through, you might ask the question if, after it goes through and leaves a telltale trace (a photon) in one slit or the other, what happens if I erase that information? Will I get the diffraction pattern again? It would be very hard, if there was a disturbance, to completely "un-disturb" it just so. But there is no disturbance here, remember? So we can ask the question, if I erase the which-slit information, can I actually get the diffraction pattern? The eraser part here is that I am going to erase the which-slit information and here is how I do it. I have these two different cavities and I take the wall out between the two of them, the two micromaser cavities, and I put a photo-absorbing plate right in between them. Remember that the rubidium atoms are left in there and they have gone through and they hit the screen. But they leave a photon, a quantum of light, in either cavity one or in cavity two. If I put a photon absorbing plate in between, then if the photon gets absorbed, I have erased the information of which side it came from. So that is how I am going to erase the information. And what I am going to do is I am going to put a set of shutters (like the shutters you have for blinds on the windows, and you can make it either shut so that the windows completely shut out the light or you can open them so the light comes through). So if we put shutters there, if the shutters are closed, I have the situation I had before where I know the which-slit information. But if I open the shutters, I give it the possibility of being erased.

And what happens here actually is that, if I do this experiment now and open the shutters, I can show that I actually get a diffraction pattern! Now this gets even stranger. So I have these rubidium atoms, they are heading toward the two-slit detector. They leave a telltale photon in one place or the other. They go through the two slits and I am going to let them already hit, completely hit the screen. Now *afterwards* I am going to decide whether or not to open the shutters and erase the information about which slit it goes through. That is called "delayed choice" mode. And if I trace the ones whose which-slit information is erased, I get a diffraction pattern. In other words, *after* the rubidium atom has already hit, I am able to determine whether or not it had behaved like a particle or a wave. In other words, whether or not it had gone through a single slit at a time, like a particle will, or gone through both slits at the same time like a wave will. *In other words, after it has already hit the screen and gone through the apparatus, I am able to determine its ontology, afterwards.*

So the point here is: how do physicists interpret this? The way physicists interpret this is by saying that we have the ability to change the past. Because I am changing how it went through the slit after it has already gone through the slits. So there is a talk about erasing what already was, restoring the diffraction pattern, and basically moving the clock backwards or changing how the particle went through after it has already gone through: *the ability to change the past*. Now I want to suggest, though, that that is a very convenient kind of nostalgic fantasy. I cannot blame physicists for engaging in this. I think this is a very seductive fantasy. Perhaps at one time or another all of us wish that we could change the past and the marks left on bodies, and change the ways in which we materialized the world, especially when we are not being careful, that we would like to undo what has been done, that we would like to go back and do it differently. But is this really what this experiment is telling us about what is possible?

It turns out that if we look at this experiment more carefully—it is all explained in Chapter 7—the original diffraction pattern is *not* being restored whatsoever and there is no complete erasure going on here at all. What is happening here is that the experiment is not about engaging a past that already was. See, we assume that time is a given externality, just a parameter that marches forward, and that the past already happened and the present, that moment "now" just slipped away into the past, and that the future is yet to come. But if we examine this carefully, again using the insights from feminist theory, from post-structuralist theory, and things that Cultural Studies has been telling us, and so on, and bring them into the physics here, what we can see is that what is going on actually is *the making of temporality*. There are questions of temporality that are coming to the fore here. What we are seeing here is that time is not given, it is not universally given, but rather that time is articulated and re-synchronized through various material practices. In other words, just like position, momentum, wave and particle, *time itself* only makes sense in the context of particular phenomena. So what is going on here is that physicists are actually making time in marking time, and that there is a certain way in which what we take to be the "past" and what we take to be the "present" and the "future" are entangled with one another. What we have learned from this experiment is that what exists are intra-active entanglements. That is the only reason we get a diffraction pattern again, by the way.

And importantly, the original diffraction pattern doesn't return, a new one is created, one in which the diffraction (that is, entanglement effects) is a bit challenging to trace. So, the issue is not one of erasure and return. What is at issue is an entanglement, intra-activity. The "past" was never simply there to begin with, and the "future" is not what will unfold, but "past" and "future" are iteratively reconfigured and enfolded through the world's ongoing intra-activity. There is no inherently determinate relationship between past, present, and future. In rethinking causality as intra-activity and not as this kind of billiard-ball causality—cause followed by an effect—the fantasy of erasure is not possible, but possibilities for reparation exist. That "changing the past" in the sense of undoing certain discrete moments in time is an illusion. The past, like the future though, is not closed. But "erasure" is not what is at issue. In an important sense, the "past" is open to change. It can be redeemed, productively reconfigured in an iterative unfolding of spacetimematter. But its sedimenting effects, its trace, can not be erased. The memory of its materializing effects is written into the world. So changing the past is never without costs, or responsibility. A recent Ph.D. student of mine, Astrid Schrader (whose work is really remarkable, well worth looking out for) has an amazing paper in *Social Studies of Science* entitled "Responding to *Pfiesteria piscicida* (the Fish Killer): Phantomatic Ontologies, Indeterminacy, and Responsibility in Toxic Microbiology" (2010), showing how previously incompatible experiments on a tiny aquatic organism with large environmental policy stakes can be reconciled by tracing how time is differently made/synchronized through different laboratory practices. She argues that memory is not a matter of the past, but recreates the past each time it is invoked.

What I am trying to make clear is—all of this is an answer to your question, believe it or not—a sample of what I have learned from engaging with quantum physics that helps me further my understanding of feminist issues and practices. My passion for my work is utterly and completely grounded, and hopefully always with its feet attached to the ground, in questions of justice and ethics. This is what totally drives me. So I think there is a way in which the physics here actually helps me to bring an important materialist sense to Derridean notions of justice-to-come. That is not justice which we presume we know what it is in advance and which is forever fixed. So just to end this short answer with a couple of quotes from Derrida:

> [The concern is] not with horizons of modified—past or future—presents, but with a "past" that has never been present, and which never will be, whose future to come will never be a *production* or a reproduction in the form of presence (Derrida [1968] 1982, 21; original emphasis).

And furthermore that:

> No justice [...] seems possible or thinkable without the principle of some *responsibility*, beyond all living present, within that

which disjoins the living present, before the ghosts of those who
are not yet born or who are already dead [...]. Without this
non-contemporaneity with itself of the living present [...] without
this responsibility and this respect for justice concerning those
who *are not there*, of those who are no longer or who are not yet
present and living, what sense would there be to ask the question
"where?" "where tomorrow?" "whither?" (Derrida [1993] 2006,
xviii; original emphasis).

So this is an example of what I learned from my diffractive engagements with physics: what responsibility entails in our active engagement of sedimenting out the world in certain kinds of ways and not others. Being attentive to ways in which we are re-doing, with each intra-action materially re-doing the material configurings of spacetimemattering. The past and the present and the future are always being reworked. And so that says that the phenomena are diffracted and temporally and spatially distributed across multiple times and spaces, and that our responsibility to questions of social justice have to be thought about in terms of a different kind of causality. It seems very important to me to be bringing physics to feminism as well as feminism to physics. (To understand my response as something learned from physics and applied to feminism is to have misunderstood something fundamental about what I am trying to say.)

Q5: A lot of scholars within the Humanities have great difficulties with posthumanist theories especially because they seem to lack an ethics, and you already talked about ethics. Especially when you bring in physics, this critique will no doubt be even stronger. At several moments in your work, however, one gets the impression that the ethics implicit in your approach is of great importance to you, as you already mentioned. Obviously when one wants to be part of feminist debates, it is impossible not *to articulate onto-epistemology as an* ethico-onto-epistemology. *In your "Posthumanist Performativity: Toward an Understanding of How Matter Comes to Matter" (Barad 2003) your emphasis on the material-discursive seems to critique the idea of the "medium." This idea seems to claim that there are cases in which meaning can be non-material, idealistically traveling through space while not being affected by matter, actually remaining ultimately "the same," or unaltered. Your texts show that this idea of the medium is in conflict with the argument that matter and meaning are necessarily entangled.*

Our question then would be how to understand this relational ontology that rejects the metaphysics of what used to be called "relata," of words and things. How is an ethics at work in how matter comes to matter?

KB: I think that you can already probably see from what I have been saying that I believe that questions of ethics and of justice are always already threaded through the very fabric of the world. They are not an additional concern that gets added on or placed in our field of vision now and again by particular kinds of concern. Being is threaded through with mattering. Epistemology, ontology, and ethics are inseparable. Matters of fact, matters of concern, and matters of care are shot through with one another. Or to put it in yet another way: matter and meaning cannot be severed. In my agential realist account, matter is a dynamic expression/articulation of the world in its intra-active becoming. All bodies, including but not limited to human bodies, come to matter through the world's iterative intra-activity, its performativity. Boundaries, properties, and meanings are differentially enacted through the intra-activity of mattering. Differentiating is not about radical exteriorities (we saw that in the experiments I just talked about) but rather what I call agential separability. That is, differentiating is not about Othering, separating, but on the contrary, about making connections and commitments. So the very nature of materiality itself is an entanglement. Hence, what is on the other side of the agential cut is never separate from us. Agential separability is not individuation. Ethics is therefore not about right responses to a radically exteriorized other, but about responsibility and accountability for the lively relationalities of becoming, of which we are a part. Ethics is about mattering, about taking account of the entangled materializations of which we are part, including new configurations, new subjectivities, new possibilities. Even the smallest cuts matter. Responsibility, then, is a matter of the ability to respond. Listening for the response of the other and an obligation to be responsive to the other, who is not entirely separate from what we call the self. This way of thinking ontology, epistemology, and ethics together makes for a world that is always already an ethical matter.

Q6: Finally, if you then propose a materialist ethics through physics, similar to the way people like Badiou (2007) and Meillassoux ([2006] 2008) re-absolutize the scope of mathematics, you indeed stir up post-Kantian academia. This has to have consequences for how you value various disciplines. Not falling into the traps of disciplinarity, multi-disciplinarity, inter-disciplinarity, or post-disciplinarity, how would you then qualify your manifesto for academic research?

KB: Well, manifesto is a thing that my friend and colleague Donna Haraway can get into, but I cannot claim that term. [Laughs.] Of course, she means it ironically. Agential realism is not a manifesto, it does not take for granted that all is or will or can be made manifest. On the contrary, it is a call, a plea, a provocation, a cry, a passionate yearning for an appreciation of, attention to the tissue of ethicality that runs through the world. Ethics and justice are at the core of my concerns or rather, it runs through "my" very being, all being. Again, for me, ethics is not a concern we add to the questions of matter, but rather is the very nature of what it means to matter.

Notes

1. This text is the result of an intra-active event ("Meeting Utrecht Halfway") that took place on June 6, 2009 at the *7th European Feminist Research Conference*, hosted by the Graduate Gender Programme of Utrecht University. The authors would like to thank the Center for Adaptive Optics at the University of California, Santa Cruz and the Infrastructurele Dienst Centrumgebied at Utrecht University for providing the video conferencing facilities, Heleen Klomp for transcribing the event, and the audience in Utrecht (esp. Magdalena Gorska, Sami Torssonen, and Alice Breemen) and Santa Cruz (esp. Karen's partner Fern Feldman and her canine companion Bina who were willing to sit through a transcontinental interview well before the sun came up on the west coast of the U.S.) for attending.
2. *Science, Technology, and the Humanities: A New Synthesis*, April 24-25, 2009.

Chapter 4

"There is contingent being independent of us, and this contingent being has no reason to be of a subjective nature"
Interview with Quentin Meillassoux

Q1: Your debut book After Finitude *([2006] 2008) is considered by many to be one of the fiercest attacks on the history of modern thought, critiquing its humanism, its immanent metaphysics, its anti-materialism.[1] You rigorously develop what you refer to as speculative materialism by means of rewriting this history, or as you refer to it, by rewriting correlationism. This term is conceptualized throughout the book and has certainly triggered many scholars—sometimes referred to as the speculative realists (see Bryant et al, eds. 2011)—to develop a new philosophy of science and a new view on how move away from Kant. Correlationism, which you refer to as "the idea according to which we only ever have access to the correlation between thinking and being, and never to either term considered apart from the other" (Meillassoux [2006] 2008, 5) is severely critiqued by others who use this term. For you, however, the correlationist standpoint deserves great respect, which you do not just critique, but rather "radicalize from within: as an 'inside job,'" as Harman (2011a, 25) puts it.*

In this book, which is mapping what we refer to as a new materialism, we felt no need to include or exclude particular scholars, and thus we also see no reason to count you in (or out). What we do notice is that we outline a similar trajectory to your own, albeit that these trajectories are developed in very different ways. Can you give us a rough sketch of the path you have been taking, giving much attention to this most complex idea of "correlationism"?

Quentin Meillassoux: In my book I frontally oppose two positions: a) "strong correlationism" which, in my opinion, is the most rigorous form of *anti*-absolutism, and therefore of contemporary *anti*-metaphysics, and b) a metaphysics I call "subjective," which, *conversely*, is nowadays the most widespread philosophy of the absolute, one which consists in posing this or that feature of the subject as essentially necessary—that is, its status as part of a correlate.

Let us specify this distinction. In chapter 1 of *After Finitude*, I define correlationism in general as an anti-absolutist thesis: one uses the correlate "subject-object" (broadly defined) as an instrument of refutation of all metaphysics to enforce that we would have access to a modality of the in-itself. Instead, for correlationism, we cannot access any form of the in-itself, because we are irremediably confined in our relation-to-the-world, without any means to verify whether the reality that is given to us corresponds to reality taken in itself, independently of our subjective link to it. For me, there are two main forms of correlationism: weak and strong (see chapter 2, p. 42 for the announcement of this difference and p. 48 ff. for its explanation). Weak correlationism is identified with Kant's transcendental philosophy: it is "weak" in that it still grants too much to the speculative pretension (e.g. absolutory) of thought. Indeed, Kant claims that we know something exists in itself, and that it is thinkable (non-contradictory). "Strong" correlationism does not even admit that we can know that there is an "in-itself" and that it can be thought: for this we are radically confined in our thought, without the possibility of knowing the in-itself, not even its taking place and logicity.

I then define correlationism's most rigorous contemporary opponent: the subjectivist metaphysician. The one who believes, unlike the strong correlationist (let's call him simply "the correlationist" from now on), that we *can* actually access an absolute: that of the correlate. Instead of saying, like the correlationist, that we can not access the in-itself because we are confined to the correlate, the subjectivist metaphysician (let's call him the "subjectivist" alone) asserts that the in-itself is the correlate itself.

Thus the "subjectivist's" thesis, according to its various instances, absolutizes various features of subjectivity. We have seen this from Hegel's speculative idealism, which absolutizes Reason, to the various actual variations of vitalism (along the dominant Nietzsche/Deleuze axis) that absolutize will, perception, affect, et cetera. For me, Deleuze is a metaphysical subjectivist who has absolutized a set of features of subjectivity, hypostatized as Life (or "a Life"), and has posed them as radically independent of our human and individual relationship to the world.

This distinction between strong correlationism and subjectivist metaphysics constitutes the very core of the book. Chapter 3, in fact, lays the foundation of my enterprise. Chapter 3 is entirely based on the clash between correlationism and subjectivism, and it is that confrontation that allows me to establish the absolute necessity of facticity—a point of view from which you must read all my subsequent positions.

Q2: In your view Deleuze, who has made important contributions to what we refer to as "new materialism," is not materialist because the absolute primacy of the unseparated ("nothing can be unless it is some form of relation to the world") in his metaphysics does not allow for the Epicurean atom "which has neither intelligence, nor will, nor life" (Meillassoux [2006] 2008, 37) to be possible. Though it should be added that the Deleuze (with and without Guattari) is important to your thinking and still demands more thinking (Meillassoux 2010). You emphasize that science and mathematics have posed questions to philosophy (questions concerning the ancestral) that demand a speculative materialism freed from the primacy of the unseparated. Yet how can you simultaneously claim to break with a transcendental statement such as: what is asubjective cannot be—and yet marry a similar approach to that of Kant concerning science or mathematics?

QM: Let's be precise again. The statement: "what is asubjective cannot be" is the only "common point" of both anti-metaphysical correlationism and subjectivist metaphysics. But we must understand in what way and to what extent. For the correlationist, it means that I can never think the object by doing the economy of my subjective point of view. For the correlationist, the statement therefore means: the a-subjective is unthinkable for us ("it cannot be" means: "it cannot be *thinkable*"). For the subjectivist the statement conversely means that the a-subjective is absolutely impossible: "it cannot be" = "it cannot be in itself." Metaphysics of Life or of Spirit, transcendental philosophy, or strong correlationism: all converge in the denunciation of "naïve realism" proper to an Epicurean type of materialism asserting that some non-subjective exists (atoms and void) and that we can know it. I really break with this anti-realist consensus, notably with any form of transcendental, and yet without going back to Epicureanism, which in its genre still remained a metaphysics (not subjective but realist) because it supported the real need for atoms and void.

But this certainly does not prevent me from maintaining the demand for an elucidation of science's conditions of thinkability. Such a demand, in fact, has nothing transcendental in itself: it is proper to any philosophy which seeks to know what it is speaking of when using the term "science." My thesis is that we still do not understand what this word means, since we failed to resolve the aporia of the arche-fossil: that the mathematized sciences of nature are only thinkable under the conditions of granting an absolute scope to its statements, an absolute scope that all anti-metaphysical philosophies of the era have challenged. Subjectivist metaphysics could rightly assert that they have maintained the absolute scope of thought and that they therefore do not fall under the problem of arche-fossil: however, I show that these metaphysics are effectively refuted by strong correlationism, and that consequently they are also ultimately unable to resolve this aporia.

Q3: Perhaps we should talk about why we should rewrite the history of thought. Many authors interested in developing a materialist or realist philosophy today are keen on rejecting humanism because of its (implicit) representationalist or linguisticist theorizations, claiming that in this emphasis on the copy or on language a lethal reductivism has entered thought (in philosophy and the humanities more generally, but in the sciences just as well). You, on the other hand, intend to break open correlationist thinking in order to reach out for the Absolute again. Many will agree with you that the Absolute has been excluded from thinking more and more since the coming of modernity (since the rise of Kant-inspired correlationism, to use your terms). In fact, whereas Nietzsche famously claimed at the end of the 19th century (in Also Sprach Zarathustra *([1883–1885] 1967)) that critical thinking had killed God, you claim the exact opposite: because of correlationism the Absolute has become unthinkable. Critiquing Kant through Descartes and Hume especially when it comes down to causality, you intend to push correlationism to the extreme, revealing what you refer to as the Principle of Facticity: a radically different conceptualization of nature (nature as contingent) and its relation to thinking. Radicalizing (weak) correlationism shows us that, as you put it "every world is without reason, and is thereby capable* of actually becoming otherwise without reason" (Meillassoux [2006] 2008, 53; original emphasis).

QM: Let me explain this point again in a few words. The subjectivist asserts that the correlationist discovered, in spite of him, the true absolute: not a reality outside of the correlate, but the correlate as such. Indeed, the correlationist has demonstrated that we could not claim to think of a reality independent of the correlation without immediately contradicting ourselves: to think the in-itself is to think it, thus making it a correlate of our subjective activity of thought instead of making it an absolute independent of us. But this, according to the subjectivist, demonstrates that this absolute is nothing other than the correlation itself. Because, by the correlationist's own confession, I cannot conceive the correlate's disappearance or being-other without immediately reconducting it in its own structures, which means that in reality I cannot think the correlation otherwise than as necessary. This conclusion contradicts the correlationist's anti-absolutist thesis. However the subjectivist nevertheless extracts it from the argument of the correlationist, thus turning correlationism against itself: the correlate, instrument of *de-absolutization* of realist metaphysics, is turned back into an anti-realist absolute. But the strong correlationist has not yet spoken his last word: in Chapter 3, I show that in his most contemporary forms (Heidegger or Wittgenstein) he manages to refute the subjective response by opposing the irreducible facticity to the *absolutization* of the correlation. I shall let you re-read how I describe this answer: the conclusion I draw upon is that strong correlationism cannot be refuted by the absolutization of the correlation as believed by the subjectivist, but rather by the absolutization of facticity (wherein resides the meaning of the principle of factuality).

Q4: *Though you mention several times that* speculative materialism *is in search of a diachronic approach, your use of concepts does point us to a time (and place) long gone (the arche-fossil for instance). Also when you state that "[...] there is a deeper level of temporality, with which what came before the relation-to-the-world is itself but a modality of that relation-to-the-world" (ibid., 123), this depth, which comes back several times in the final chapter, should be searched for "before" thought. This reminds us once again of a Heideggerian approach which intends to take us "back" to the things themselves. Now as we've seen before, you are in fact quite critical of Heidegger (not only in your answer above but also for instance* on ibid., 41–2, where you accuse him (together with Wittgenstein) of setting up a strong correlationism that dominated twentieth century philosophy). Though you quote mainly his later work, your critique of Heidegger focuses primarily on questions of being that were more central to his earlier work. In his Die Frage nach Technik *(1954)* and also in Der Ursprung des Kunstwerkes *(1960)* we can easily read a materialism that comes close to yours as he too questions relationality and is in search of a more complete and deeper meaning of things (and times) that can be found only before this relationality came into being.

Speculatively taking away the idealist and sometimes humanist dimension of Heidegger's thinking, could we say that the phenomenological notion of going back to the things themselves, and also their interest in **rewriting**, as Lyotard *([1988] 1991)* would put it, ancient Greek thinking (think as well of your last chapter entitled "Ptolemy's Revenge") is also your interest? Or would you at least share his idea not so much of rewriting a pre-human, but rather a pre-modern or classical philosophy?

QM: In relation to Heidegger, I take care to show that he has in fact never escaped correlationism, neither in his later nor in his earlier period. That is why I quote his *Identity and Difference* (chapter 1, p. 41–2), which brings back *Ereignis*—a central notion from *after* the "turn" in Heidegger's work—to a clearly correlational structure. The "return to things themselves," which was the slogan of Husserl's phenomenology before that of the early Heidegger, in no way corresponds to my idea of philosophy: as it only consists, by this call, in returning to the things as correlates of consciousness, Dasein, phenomenon, being, or Being. If the given were the thing in itself, then the thing would intrinsically be something given-to, but according to me, this is not the case. There is therefore no return to "things in themselves," but rather to the in-itself seen as indifferent to what is given to us, because indifferent to our opening-the-world.

I am not involved in a return to or a rewriting of the Greeks—such an enterprise offers no determinate meaning to my approach.

Q5: Michel Foucault was the first to announce the End of Man or the second Copernican turn in The Order of Things *([1966] 1970). His new way of writing history might not have excluded the human mind, but certainly it at least claims not to start with it. His idea of discourse for instance did not start with language, but with material forms (for instance the prison-form) which came along with expressive forms like delinquency (which is not a signifier, but part of a set of statements reciprocally presupposing the material form of the prison). To push this a bit further, it seems not too difficult to rephrase this argument without the human mind playing even a minor role in it. Think for instance of how sedimentary processes work, where pebbles are picked up by water streams (expressed through them) and are sorted in uniform layers creating the new entity of the sedimentary rock (new substances), a non-linear and ongoing process also in movement because of tectonic movements, weather conditions and much more (complicated) processes of change that in the end create movements very similar to how Foucault saw them taking place in respect to nineteenth century processes of delinquency.*

In what way then is your approach different from Foucault's? Or, where is the arche-fossil different and less dependent upon the human mind than the pebbles in the example above?

QM: Concerning Foucault I will simply answer as follows. His investigation focuses on past dispositives of knowledge-power, and eventually on dispositives that are contemporary to him. He can bring us nothing in regards to the disqualification of strong correlationism, because the disqualification is situated at a level that his research does not address, but rather presupposes. Indeed, I examine how correlationism, from its point of departure in the Cogito, has come to dominate all of modern thought, including the most resolutely anti-Cartesian: the "great confinement" was not that of the fools in the asylum, but that of the philosophers in the Correlate—and this also applies to Foucault. Indeed, Foucault does not say anything that would embarrass a correlationist, as all his comments can easily be considered as a discourse-correlated-to-the-point-of-view-of-our-time, and rigorously dependent on it. This is a typical thesis of some correlationist relativism: we are trapped in our time, not in Hegelian terms, but rather in a Heideggerian fashion—that is to say in the modality of knowledge-power that always already dominates us. His thesis on the "disappearance of man" is about man understood as an object of "human sciences," not about the correlate as I conceive it.

I am not at all hostile to Foucault's thesis, even though in my view he thinks within a historicist ontology that remains unthought in its deep nature—even in his magnificent course entitled "Society Must be Defended" (Foucault 2003).

Q6: The central question of your book was: How is thought able to think what there can be when there is no thought? (Meillassoux [2006] 2008, 36) A lot of scholars in the humanities, though sympathetic to your re-reading of Kant and Hume, might not see the urgency of this question. Feminism for instance might be interested in thinking beyond the male-female dichotomy and contemporary feminist theory would also definitely not start its analysis from the human (female) mind, but the urgency of thinking a place without thought would probably be considered the pointless question par excellence, as you already phrased it (ibid., 121). How would you suggest convincing them?

QM: That the question of what there is when there is no thought is considered by many—and not only by feminists—as devoid of meaning or interest is indeed likely. As you recall, I specifically say: the problem is to understand how the most urgent question has come to be regarded as the most idle one. The question is not about convincing anyone to think otherwise, because it is a very strong feature of our era that we cannot fight in a few sentences.

If I had to say something to shake actual certainties, I would formulate it in a provocative fashion, but basically this is what I think: I assert that anyone who refuses to deal with this question simply does not know what he is saying when he utters the words "science," "mathematics," "absolute," "metaphysics," "non-metaphysics," and other words of equal significance. What I say in my book and in the lines above suffice to explain what allows me to say that.

That is why the question of sexual difference cannot be foreign to this interrogation. For instance, Lacan's entire work is crossed by the question of the scientificity or non-scientificity of psychoanalysis, and finds one of its points of culmination in the notion of the "matheme." Well, I argue for any Lacanian discourse—which is admittedly related to the question of the difference between "man/woman" or "male/female"—to be unable to grasp the meaning of its most crucial concepts until it will not have treated as its necessary prerequisite the question of the non-correlational in science. The same also applies to any feminist theory that incorporates in its discourse one of the terms quoted above.

Q7: You shift strong correlationism by revolutionizing Kant and Hume, thus by demonstrating how a radical anti-anthropocentrism fulfills the Copernican revolution. Central to this radical anti-anthropocentrism by which you re-absolutize thought is mathematics *(ibid., 101, 103, 113, 126)*: *"what is mathematizable cannot be reduced to a correlate of thought" (ibid., 117). This entails a definite move away from thinking science philosophically, because this is what has obfuscated "science's non-correlational mode of knowing, in other words, its eminently speculative character" (ibid., 119; original emphasis). What you state is that of the statement "thought can think that event X can actually have occurred prior to all thought, and indifferently to it," "no variety of correlationism [...] can admit that that statement's literal meaning is also its deepest meaning" (ibid., 122; original emphasis). In line with the argument it makes sense to link this eternal truth that we find in mathematics to a "realism" (albeit speculative), but how could we call it a materialism? Is the morphogenetic dynamics of mathematics equal to matter?*

QM: I intend to demonstrate–note here that this is still not done in *After Finitude*—that what is mathematizable is absolutizable. You ask me if this is a materialist thesis rather than a merely "realist" one. It is difficult to discuss the relevance of my thesis if we omit the whole discussion of the problem of the arche-fossil found in Chapter 1. I will nevertheless answer as follows: for me, materialism holds in two key statements: 1. Being is separate and independent of thought (understood in the broad sense of subjectivity), 2. Thought can think Being. Thesis number 1 is opposed to any anthropomorphism which seeks to extend subjective attributes to Being: materialism is not a form of animism, spiritualism, vitalism, etcetera. It asserts that non-thinking actually precedes, or at least may in right precede thought, and exists outside of it, following the example of Epicurean atoms, devoid of any subjectivity, and independent of our relationship to the world. Thesis number 2 affirms that materialism is rationalism (again broadly defined as there are different definitions of reason) in that it is always an enterprise that, through skepticism, opposes an activity of knowledge and criticism to religious appeal, to mystery, or to the limitation of our knowledge.

Skepticism and faith converge in the thesis of our finitude, making us available to any belief: conversely, materialism grants the human being the capacity to think by his own means the truth of both his environment and condition. Under the enemy of reason, he always knows how to detect the priest. He also knows that no one has more desire to be right—without allowing one to argue against him—than the opponent of reason.

I follow these two theses because I argue and demonstrate—strictly through argumentation—that there is contingent being independent of us, and furthermore, that this contingent being has no reason to be of a subjective nature. I also try to found a scientific rationalism based on the use of mathematics to describe non-human and inorganic reality. This is not to "Pythagorize," or to assert that Being is inherently mathematical: it is rather to explain how it is that a formal language manages to capture, from contingent-Being, properties that a vernacular language fails at restituting. My thesis on mathematics is a thesis on the scope of formal languages, not a thesis on Being. I do not posit it by whim or "scientist" tropism, but because I showed with the problem of arche-fossil that there one had no choice: if the sciences have meaning, then mathematics has an absolute scope. Yet sciences have meaning, and hence sciences rest via their mathematized formulations on a reality that is radically independent of our humanity. This contrasts with the 'qualitative' judgments of ordinary perception, which can safely be thought for their part as correlated to the sensible relation we have with the world, and as having no existence outside of this relation. The absolute scope of mathematics must therefore be established, and our only way to do this is, I think, is to pass through the derivative scope of the principle of factuality. This is the problem left out in *After Finitude*: a problem that simultaneously traces the program of a consequent speculative materialism.

Q8: In your conceptualization of potentiality vs. virtuality you note that potentiality comes with a determined world, conforming to the laws of nature. Superchaos, on the other hand, comes with virtuality. How is thinking the virtual linked to speculation, and what role is there for matter (and nature)? We ask the latter sub-question, because we noticed that whereas on page 11 you speak of matter, life, thought and justice, on page 14 you only speak of the latter three. We introduced the concept of nature in reference to your apparent affinity with Spinoza's physics (not with his metaphysics).

Finally, then, the vectorial subject to be developed in speculative materialism does not emancipate but rather anticipates the unforeseen, though in keeping with the law of non-contradiction. Doing away with idealism, it would be most interesting to see how this emancipation "does not yet exist," especially in relation to how it then affirms or critiques the great French feminists like Cixous and even de Beauvoir, when they emphasize not so much a final emancipation but rather the willingness to write or think femininity.

QM: For me, matter is not identifiable with "nature." Nature is a world order determined by specific constants, and that determines within itself this set of possibles that I call "potentialities." In return, matter is a primordial ontological order: it is the fact that there must be something and not nothing—contingent beings as such. One can imagine an infinity and more of material worlds governed by different laws: they would be different "natures," although equally material. Matter's second characteristic is negative: it designates contingent non-living and non-thinking beings. In our world, life and thought are constituted on a background of inorganic matter to which they return. One could perhaps imagine a nature entirely alive or spiritual in which case "matter" would be pushed out—but it would remain an essential and eternal possibility of Superchaos because every nature can be destroyed by it, but not the contingent being in a state of pure-material.

Concerning the theory of the materialist subject, I am indeed interested in challenging the identification of action with its pure present deployment, while simultaneously repeating the criticism of the former revolutionary model of future emancipation. However, I think that the present is intimately constituted by the "projection" of the subject to this not-yet-present. Here I am not saying anything original: Heidegger as well as Sartre has insisted on this constitutive dimension of the future in the constitution of the subjective present. However, I add a very different dimension to this projection: a dimension which is not only devoid of religious transcendence, but also inaccessible to the subject's action—an articulation that I believe effective of radical egalitarian justice (of the living and of the dead) and the eternal return as proof of return (a resurrection intensely deceptive). What interests me is the feedback effect of this expectation on the present of action and on the concrete transformation of the subject.

Notes

1. Translation (from the French) by Marie-Pier Boucher.

II
Cartographies

Introduction
A "New Tradition" in Thought

Chapter 5 ("The Transversality of New Materialism") focuses on three ways in which new materialism can be called "transversal." So far we have seen that new materialism is a cultural theory that does not privilege matter over meaning or culture over nature. It explores a *monist* perspective, devoid of the dualisms that have dominated the humanities (and sciences) until today, by giving special attention to matter, which has been so neglected by dualist thought. Cartesian dualism, after all, has favored mind. As concerns feminist literary theory in the deconstructive paradigm, for instance, it has been noted that:

> Men have aligned the opposition male/female with rational/ emotional, serious/frivolous, or reflective/spontaneous, [whereas] feminist criticism [...] works to prove itself more rational, serious, and reflective than male readings that omit and distort (Culler [1982] 2008, 58).

It is this kind of scholarship, according to Jonathan Culler, but also according to DeLanda (as seen in the interview above) that attempts to provoke a shift in thought, but which continues the dominant scholarly mode of thinking. And whereas this act of reclaiming thought has been important for feminism, it has not spurred a revolution in thought (as we will explain in Chapters 5 and 7). New materialism wants to set such a revolution in motion, and for this reason it has a renewed interest in philosophical monism or in the philosophy of immanence. New materialism, as a transversally new intellectual orientation, works through the transcendental and humanist (dualist) traditions that haunt cultural theory, and finds itself transversally on the brink of both the modern *and* the post-postmodern eras. The transcendental and humanist traditions, despite being manifold, are consistently predicated on dualist structures. New materialists open up the paradoxes inherent in those traditions by creating concepts that traverse the fluxes of matter and mind, body and soul, nature and culture, and opens up active theory formation. The three transversalities discussed in Chapter 5 concern disciplinarity, paradigms, and the spatiotemporality of theory—that is, the cartographical methodology introduced in the interview with Braidotti.

Chapter 6 ("Pushing Dualism to an Extreme") discusses the way in which new materialism constitutes a philosophy of difference or immanence by working through or "traversing" the dualisms that form the backbone of modernist thought. This chapter dives immediately into the epistemological or even *methodological* dimension of new materialism itself as displayed by the interviewees in Part One. Continuing the transversal ideas of Lyotard, Deleuze, and Bruno Latour about the temporality of theory formation, new materialists have set themselves to a rewriting of all *possible and impossible* forms of emancipation. This rewriting exercise involves a movement in thought that, in the words of Henri Bergson ([1896] 2004, 236), can be termed "push[ing] dualism to an extreme." By this movement, Deleuze ([1968] 1994, 45) has stated that "difference is pushed to the limit," that is to say, "difference" is "shown *differing*" (ibid., 68; emphasis in original). The chapter addresses the new materialist ways in which modernity's dualisms (structured by a negative relation between terms) are traversed, and how a new conceptualization of difference (structured by an affirmative relation) comes to be constituted along the way. This conceptualization of difference leaves behind all prioritizations (implicitly) involved in modern dualist thinking, since a difference structured by affirmation does not work with predetermined relations (e.g. between mind and body) nor does it involve a counter-hierarchy between terms. The chapter makes explicit the *methodology* of the current-day rise of non-dualist thought, both in terms of its non-classificatory mode of (Deleuzian) thinking, and in terms of the theory of the time of thought thus effectuated (Lyotard's notion of "rewriting modernity" is not a postmodernism). We conclude by demonstrating how this new materialism traverses the sexual dualisms that structure modernist feminist thinking, anticipating the next chapter that includes a re-reading of Simone de Beauvoir's *The Second Sex* ([1949] 2010), mainly through the work of Elizabeth Grosz. This short demonstration forms the bridge to Chapter 7.

The seventh chapter ("Sexual Differing") envisions a new way of mapping the relations between the sexes by moving beyond sex, sexual difference, and gender. Instead of the epistemological groundwork for a new conceptualization of difference, this chapter is interested in new materialism's ontology of difference itself. In the dominant reception of the work of de Beauvoir, finding its apotheosis in the work of Butler, feminists overthrow sex and sexual difference in favor of gender. What we propose in a new materialist spirit is that gender, with which a revolution in thought was intended, did not produce the desired effect. Theorists of gender position themselves in dualistic opposition to theorists of sexual difference, and end up re-affirming sexual difference in its narrowest definition (the biological essentialism of sex). All forms of identity politics, as shown in the interviews summarized by the Culler citation above, involve dualism, and need to be opened up and set in motion. Counter-intuitively, a true revolution in thought does not consist of the dualistic overthrow of a seemingly outdated framework. Similar to Deleuze's rejection of Otherness that runs through a great deal of the new materialist work, we show how a revolution in thought entails the affirmation of the thinking process—that is, a practical philosophy. This chapter in line with the preceding chapter, proposes the setting up of a new materialist theory of sexual difference as a practical philosophy in which concept and creation are considered as intertwined. Re-reading de Beauvoir affirmatively, a sexual differing can be made apparent that has an eye for the material ("sex") and the discursive ("gender") in their mutual entanglement, thus shifting identity politics and biological essentialism in favor of a performative ontology, as well as the dominant conceptualization of a "revolution in thought." In the practical philosophical process, then, the present comes about as creating the past and the future: de Beauvoir (the past) is being re-read (the present), while working towards the future of feminist thought. Through our so-called case study on sex, gender, and sexual difference, we show how the new materialism is a practical philosophy that makes way for thinking metamorphoses regarding—along with sex—"race," class, and the other so-called axes of social difference.

Finally, in the eighth chapter ("The End of (Wo)Man"), we engage most directly with new materialism's new metaphysics by discussing its post-humanism or a-humanism. We start from the work of Foucault, on whose work all interviewees took a position. When Foucault in *The Order of Things* ([1966/1970] 1994) announced that man was only a recent invention, he added a permanent question mark to the humanist and modernist traditions that had dominated European thought for over two centuries. In his recently published accompanying dissertation *Introduction to Kant's Anthropology* (2008, submitted in 1961) he gives us an even more thorough perspective on how anthropocentrism has shaped our (dualist) thinking, and how it has actually distorted our strategies of studying the real. His views can definitely be considered the opening statements of new materialism, especially because Foucault in his later work has shown in so many ways how bodies (think of prisons, for instance) and the words within which they are enveloped (think of "delinquency") act only in entanglement with one another, and that the human being acts within the actualization and realization of these discursive forces. Recently, Meillassoux's *After Finitude* ([2006] 2008) proposed another re-reading of Kant that suggests that Foucault has not pushed things far enough (as Meillassoux explained in his interview).

Not even referring to Foucault in his book, Meillassoux's interests in ancestrality proposes us to think the real without it first being represented in the human mind, which, according to Meillassoux, is still the common practice in what is called post-critical theory (which probably includes Foucault). Meillassoux, continuing themes found in the early writings of Alain Badiou, together with other speculative thinkers such as Ray Brassier and Graham Harman, thus intends to fulfill Kant's Copernican revolution of the mind by proposing a radical anti-anthropocentrism, which refuses to see truth only in how it can possibly appear to the human mind. Instead, he proposes an understanding of truth (or nature) through mathematics. We will show how Meillassoux's speculative materialism differs from the positions of other prominent contemporary materialists such as Barad and

DeLanda. These authors, though also inspired by the natural sciences, emphasize that phenomena reveal themselves *from* their relations. However, we will also demonstrate how a coherence can be created between these new materialists that, after having worked through humanism and the different differences it gave rise to, asks how much (wo)man we need at all. Without intending to come to a fixed conclusion, we can see that the different developments in new materialist thinking leave us with many questions in both the sciences and the humanities on the role of the human being in the morphogenesis of the real. This book, together with the new materialist scholars it interviews and discusses, wishes to provide a methodological opening for these ontological questions.

The "new" in new materialism is not a term that accepts or continues a classificatory historiography of (academic) thinking that necessarily comes with a hierarchy or any kind of *a priori* logic. New materialism affirms that such hierachized specialization creates "minds in a groove" whereas "there is no groove of abstractions which is adequate for the comprehension of human life" (Whitehead [1925] 1997, 197). New materialism does not intend to add yet another specialized epistemology to the tree of academic knowledge production (Deleuze and Guattari [1980] 1987, 5). As such, it is thus not necessarily opposed to the crude or Historical/Marxist materialist tradition. It is not necessarily different from any other materialist, pragmatic or monist tradition either, since it carefully "works through" all these traditions in order to avoid, along with the trap of antagonism, the trap of anachronism (Lyotard [1988] 1991, 26–7) or of "a retrograde movement" (Bergson [1934] 2007, 11). New materialism says "yes, *and*" to all of these intellectual traditions, traversing them all, creating strings of thought that, in turn, create a remarkably powerful and fresh "rhythm" in academia today (Simondon [1958] 1980).

New materialism's metaphysics follows from an interdisciplinary development in thought, whose backbone is a strong interest in Continental philosophy. Yet it seems to have no difficulty in opening up these thoughts to Anglo-American thought, and actually makes their intermingling productive. Yet this is nothing "new." There are many examples in which Continental and Anglo-American thought have been moving in similar directions, as scholars were consciously or unconsciously inspired by a radical thought they felt to be present beneath what was known. After all, just like Alfred North Whitehead's plea for "wandering" through and beyond grooves (Whitehead [1925] 1997, 207), Lyotard's "working through" is "a working attached to a thought of what is constitutively hidden from us in the event and in the meaning of the event" (Lyotard [1988] 1991, 26). Or in the words of Bergson, "As though the thing and the idea of the thing, its reality and its possibility, were not created at one stroke when a truly new form, invented by art or nature is concerned!" (Bergson [1934] 2007, 11). Good ideas are never bothered by space or time. From Bergson to Whitehead and Lyotard, from Louis Hjelmslev to Benedict Spinoza, from Foucault to British Cultural Studies, and from quantum physics to contemporary feminist theory—time and again, new thoughts travel easily and have always already announced themselves when the conditions are right (De Boever et al. 2009).

One could even claim that the break between Continental and Anglo-American thought, or the divide between the sciences and the humanities as C.P. Snow ([1959] 1965) expressed it in his famous 1950 essay "The Two Cultures," were not so much states that were *noticed*, but were actually prompted by philosophers of science themselves. Snow's taxonomy *created* and eventually overcoded this radical distinction he claimed to have merely observed (cf. Kirby 2008a). Such major Historiographies, to speak again with Gilles Deleuze and Félix Guattari, are not so much critiqued by new materialism. Instead, they are being read in their relations to the minor historiographies which often result in the appearance of alternative *new* trajectories. It is in this sense that the "materialism" of new materialism is also not exclusive. It is not embraced in opposition to transcendental thinking, but instead re-reads metaphysics as a whole from a "natureculture" perspective, as science studies would call it (Latour [1991] 1993, Haraway 2003). The new materialist practice of reading as re-reading, together with the readings proposed by new materialist scholars, perform its new metaphysics.

New materialism wants to do justice to the "material-semiotic," or "material-discursive" character of *all* events, as Donna Haraway (1988, 595) and Karen Barad (2003, 810) would call it. It is interested in actualizing a metaphysics that fully affirms the active role played by matter in "receiving" a form (cf. Simondon 2009, 4). Working through Cartesian or modernist dualisms, new materialism has set itself to practice the Spinozist dictum that the mind is always already an idea of the body, while the body is the object of the mind (Spinoza [1677] 2001, E2P21, Schol.). In terms of artworks, for instance, a new materialist perspective would be interested in finding out how the form of content (the material condition of the artwork) and the form of expression (the sensations as they come about) are being produced in one another, how series of statements are actualized, and how pleats of matter are realized in the real (Deleuze and Guattari [1980] 1987, 89; cf. Bolt and Barrett eds. forthcoming). In this way, new materialism is different from most post-Kantian studies of art, since in these studies, the material and discursive dimensions are treated separately. After a short description of the materials used following a "crude materialism," the contemporary scholar influenced by the so-called "linguistic turn" proceeds to deconstruct its messages. New materialism allows for the study of the two dimensions in their entanglement: the experience of a piece of art is made up of matter *and* meaning. The material dimension creates *and* gives form to the discursive, and vice versa. Similar to what happens with the artwork, new materialism sets itself to rewriting events that are usually only of interest to natural scientists. Here it becomes apparent that a new materialist take on "nature" will be shown to be transposable to the study of "culture" and vice versa, notwithstanding the fact that these transpositions are not unilinear. After all, "transposition" is at work in music as well as genetics (Braidotti 2006, 5).

Thinking in such a way reveals to us a "[...] new form of materialist philosophy in which raw matter-energy through a variety of self-organizing processes and an intense power of morphogenesis, generates all the structures that surround us" (DeLanda 1996, n.p.). Studying these metamorphoses as they happen through the formation of content and expression, that is, through the entanglement of materiality and meaning in the widest sense of the word, new materialist thinking allows us to write such a metamorphosis not by excluding parts of it beforehand, but by at least being open to the process in its full manifestation. We need this new materialism because, whether it concerns earthquakes, art, social revolutions, or simply thinking, the material and the discursive are only taken apart in the authoritative gesture of the scholar or by the commonsensical thinker; while in the event, in life itself, the two seeming layers are by all means indiscernible. New materialism wants to move away from the authoritative scholarly attitude and from everyday utilitarian common sense, and wants to engross itself in what is "ontologically prior" (Massumi 2002, 66).

As an important but poorly defined force in contemporary academia, new materialism stands in need of conceptualization, and this second part of the book provides it. We bring together important scholars and texts that have contributed to the new materialism, and by showing the coherence in their (implicit) dialogue, by demonstrating their joint movements, we allow for a natureculture metaphysics of the ontologically prior to be actualized. But we do not map this new tradition from a distance. In this book, we add to new materialism as much as we perform a new engagement with canonical and minor academic literatures. In keeping with new materialism's interdisciplinarity, our mapping shows us how new materialist accounts are similar to certain (empirical) tendencies in accounting for nature on the one hand and cognitive accounts of culture and nature on the other.

Chapter 5
The Transversality of New Materialism

Manuel DeLanda and Rosi Braidotti—independently of one another—first started using "neo-materialism" or "new materialism" in the second half of the 1990s, for a cultural theory that does not privilege the side of culture, but focuses on what Donna Haraway (2003) would call "naturecultures" or what Bruno Latour simply referred to as "collectives" ([1991] 1993). The term proposes a cultural theory that radically rethinks the dualisms so central to our (post-)modern thinking and always starts its analysis from how these oppositions (between nature and culture, matter and mind, the human and the inhuman) are produced in action itself. It thus has a profound interest in the morphology of change and gives special attention to matter (materiality, processes of materialization) as it has been so much neglected by dualist thought. In the same breath we then always already start with the *mater*, as Braidotti (2002b, 170) already emphasized elsewhere. This explains why, along with the interest in science seen in particular with DeLanda and Latour, the emancipation of mat(t)er is also by nature a feminist project.[1]

For those familiar with the materialism of Walter Benjamin, "new materialism" is ironic for several reasons. Analyzing modernity, Benjamin ([1982] 2002, 22) rejects the modern fetish of newness and the illusions it presumes. Particularly because he considers "[n]ewness […] a quality independent of the use value of the commodity," staging a materialism that is "new" would make no sense at all. But of course there is no reason why we should confine ourselves to such a linear modernist idea of History. Especially if, in following Latour ([1991] 1993, 82), we claim that "[h]istory is no longer simply the history of people, it becomes the history of natural things as well," Benjamin's critique can be put aside. The newness we are interested in is not so much a better or improved version of "old" (historical, Marxist-inspired) materialism. DeLanda for instance has made it very clear that he rewrites this Marxism and its (humanist) take on the material (though Benjamin in particular offers us many ways out of these traps). Therefore DeLanda also wrote his famous *A Thousand Years of Nonlinear History* (1997) in which he puts such an "other" history, as proposed by Latour, to work (see also Harman 2008).

In this book it is not so much a history that is presented to the reader, but rather, following Braidotti, a *mapping* of how the materialism that is referred to as a new materialism is at work in the humanities and in the sciences at this very moment. Of course that does not mean that we exclude historicity, time, or memory; texts are read insofar as they are considered important and valuable for the non-dualist, materialist current in contemporary thought, and not judged according to when they were conceived. Thus, it is no problem to state that we see this new materialism we are interested in at work in Spinoza's *Ethics*. Benedict Spinoza, already in 1677, claims that the mind is the idea of the body, making the body necessarily the object of the mind. The mind and the body are the same thing, as he stresses repeatedly. This is a most interesting contribution to a new materialist thinking. Similarly, the present book develops an interest in the new materialist thoughts to be found in the work of the authors mentioned so far, but also in that of Simone de Beauvoir, Henri Bergson, Alfred North Whitehead and Brian Massumi, among others.

There is a good reason why a book on new materialism is written now. In recent years new materialism has proven to be capable of opposing the transcendental and humanist traditions that are haunting cultural theory, standing on the brink of the post-postmodern era. Of course dualist traditions are stubborn and have buried themselves deep in the minds of (common-sense) scholars today. These traditions continue to stir debates, which are being opened up by new materialists (think of the feminist polemic about the failed materialism in the work of Judith Butler (Kirby

2006), and of the Saussurian/ Lacanian linguistic heritage in media and cultural studies (Dolphijn 2010), which as Karen Barad (2007) has shown, have prevented the theorization of "agential matter" from being effectuated). But at the start of the 21st century, this new materialist ambition does seem to offer a more than equal alternative for scholars working in the humanities and beyond. Perhaps for the first time in its history, this "minor tradition" in thinking (as Gilles Deleuze would label it) is getting the attention it needs, freeing itself from the Platonist, Christian, and Modernist rule under which it suffered for so long.

In the work of both Braidotti and DeLanda it has been through a rethinking of several French philosophers closely connected to May '68 (including Michel Foucault, Luce Irigaray, and Gilles Deleuze and Félix Guattari) that their thinking came about. And it was the work of Deleuze (and Guattari) that was actually most important to them. Especially in his early work, Deleuze tried to show that the materialist philosophy he proposed was not new but fell into the rich though minor tradition already mentioned. By writing on philosophers like Spinoza, Nietzsche, and Bergson, but also on writers like Marcel Proust and Franz Kafka, Deleuze intended to rewrite the history of thinking by giving attention to those materialist authors it had rejected or marginalized for such a long time. At the start of his career, Deleuze puts the emphasis on re-reading radical minds like Spinoza, thus showing how they actually offer philosophy a new way of thinking—namely, a philosophy of the body. And it is by traversing these different philosophies of the body that Deleuze's other work (sometimes with Guattari) really starts exploring materialist/monist thought to the fullest, creating the fertile ground upon which new materialist scholars like Braidotti and DeLanda take root today.

Most faithful to the work of Deleuze (and Guattari), DeLanda's early version of new materialism proffered the claim that the concept "abstract machine" (Deleuze and Guattari [1980] 1987) captures processes without form of substance that can be found in concrete assemblages of biology, sociology, and geology alike, in a manner that enables cultural theory at large to move away from linguistic representationalism towards "the realm of engineering diagrams" which are "shared by very different physical assemblages. Thus there would be an "abstract motor" with different physical instantiations in technological objects and natural atmospheric processes" (DeLanda 1996, n.p.). This new materialism engenders *immanent* thought and, as a consequence, it breaks through not only the mind-matter and culture-nature divides of transcendental humanist thought, but also thinking causal structures and teleology (i.e. a determinism):

> This conception of very specific abstract machines [...] indeed points towards a new form of materialist philosophy in which raw matter-energy through a variety of self-organizing processes and an intense power of morphogenesis, generates all the structures that surround us. Furthermore, the structures generated cease to be the primary reality, and matter-energy flows now acquire this special status (ibid.).

The way in which matter seems to gain primacy in DeLanda's new materialism points instead at a "generative matter," which is a concept that does not capture matter-as-opposed-to-signification, but captures *mattering* as simultaneously material and representational (cf. Cheah 1999, Barad 2007).

Braidotti introduced new materialism or "a more radical sense of materialism" by framing it as "[r]ethinking the embodied structure of human subjectivity after Foucault" (Braidotti 2000, 158). Coming from a very rich materialist tradition in Australian feminism, Braidotti's "after Foucault" should not so much be read as a reference to a move *beyond* Foucault, given that she and DeLanda (as well as other new materialists) can be said to affirm, one way or another, the much-noted prediction of Foucault ([1970] 1998, 343) that "perhaps, one day, this century will be known as Deleuzian." Compared to DeLanda, Braidotti's new materialism is equally immanent and non-linear, and "embodied subjectivity" is conceptualized accordingly:

> A piece of meat activated by electric waves of desire, a text written by the unfolding of genetic encoding. Neither a sacralized inner *sanctum*, nor a pure socially shaped entity, the enfleshed Deleuzian subject is rather an "in-between": it is a folding-in of external influences and a simultaneous unfolding outwards of affects. A mobile entity, an enfleshed

sort of memory that repeats and is capable of lasting through sets of discontinuous variations, while remaining faithful to itself. The Deleuzian body is ultimately an embodied memory (Braidotti 2000, 159).

Apart from the immanence of the new materialism qualitatively shifting the many instantiations of cultural theory that exemplify the transcendental, there is a strong emphasis on the intra-action[2] of the technological and the natural, or as Braidotti has called it, on "the 'posthuman' predicament" which entails "much more than the definitive loss of the naturalistic paradigm" (ibid., 158). Bringing "nature" into cultural theory does not make new materialists susceptible to adopting the ontology of the so-called positivist natural sciences. One of the pillars of the new materialism is the claim that modern natural science and postmodern cultural theory are both humanisms (cf. Colebrook 2004). In Braidotti's work the shared humanist subject of biological determinism and social constructivism is exchanged for a *post-humanist subject*, which entails for starters a qualitative shift away from the two poles of present-day epistemology: positivism and postmodernism (cf. Haraway 1988).

In their subsequent work, DeLanda and Braidotti continued constituting new materialism by posing *dual oppositions* as their main target. Reworking and eventually *breaking through* dualism appears to be the key to new materialism. Dualism comes to the fore as the structuring principle of the transcendental and humanist traditions that they want to shift in their work. Prioritizing mind over matter or culture over nature is a transcendentalizing gesture following humanist and dialecticist thought. It posits postmodernism as overcoming the flaws of positivism, and social constructivism as overcoming biological determinism. As such, the gesture is predicated upon sequential negation, and has a progress narrative structure. The reliance upon dialecticism has been uncovered as an effect of what Lynn Hankinson Nelson (1993, 127–8) termed "unreal dichotomies" or "non-exhaustive oppositions." Nelson has made clear that one pole of a dichotomy or binary opposition is always already implied in the other *as its negation*, which makes dichotomies unreal and oppositions non-exhaustive. In the words of Michel Serres:

> An idea opposed to another idea is always the same idea, albeit affected by the negative sign. The more you oppose one another, the more you remain in the same framework of thought (Serres with Latour 1995, 81).

The intimate relation between two so-called opposites makes it clear that the transcendental and humanist tendencies, which are fought by new materialist theorists are fundamentally reductive. After all, negation implies a relation, which is precisely what is undone by the dependence of transcendental humanist thought on dualism.

Attempting to break through reductive dualist thought in *A New Philosophy of Society*, DeLanda (2006, 45–6; original emphasis) makes the following statement:

> [...] general categories do not refer to anything in the real world and [...] to believe they do (i.e. to reify them) leads directly to essentialism. Social constructivism is supposed to be an antidote to this, in the sense that by showing that general categories are mere stereotypes it blocks the move towards their reification. But by coupling the idea that perception is intrinsically linguistic with the ontological assumption that only the contents of experience really exist, this position leads directly to a form of *social essentialism*.

Linguisticality (which is *not denied*, but given its proper place, that is, a more modest one) forms the nexus of DeLanda's non-dualist argument about new materialism. *Anti-representationalism* (an immanent gesture) is employed so as to break through the assumed binary opposition between realist essentialism and social constructivism. Due to the fact that causally linear, predetermined and constrained reasoning has been left behind (or at least is included in an open, constrained yet undecidable[3] notion of causality that fills up all of its dimensions), it cannot be argued that new materialism entails a simple move *beyond* social constructivism in a progressive way. According to DeLanda, new materialism is *neither* realist *nor* social constructivist. It is precisely the commonalities of realism and social constructivism that are being recognized, though shifted.

Braidotti (2006, 130; cf. Rossini 2006) theorizes similar moves in *Transpositions*, yet with a clear focus on feminist politics:

> In the political economy of phallologocentrism and of anthropocentric humanism, which predicates the sovereignty of Sameness in a falsely universalistic mode, my sex fell on the side of 'Otherness,' understood as pejorative difference, or as being-worth-less-than. The becoming-animal/ becoming-world speaks to my feminist self, partly because my gender, historically speaking, never quite made it into full humanity, so my allegiance to that category is at best negotiable and never to be taken for granted.
>
> This is neither an essentialist statement, nor one of semiotic constructivism. It is rather the materialist acknowledgement of a historical location: a starting position of asymmetrical power differentials. This location is not only geopolitical, but also genealogical and time-bound.

Braidotti's claim is anti-representationalist in two ways. First of all, she cuts across a biological (or Platonic) essentialism and "semiotic constructivism" (here, a relativism) in a manner that mirrors DeLanda. Secondly, a feminist politics is conceptualized, which does not embrace the dualist move of creating counter-identities (a modernist feminist project) nor does it attempt to move beyond dualism by producing a plethora of counter-identities according to a pluralizing gesture (a postmodernist feminist project, and again a relativism). Feminists "rather go further and push towards qualitatively stronger de-territorializations" (ibid., 134), that is, towards becoming-animal/becoming-world, which entails a breakthrough of the naturalizing tendencies of both sexist humanism *and* the de-naturalizing tendencies of modern and postmodern feminisms.

What we find in the work of DeLanda and Braidotti is a series of moves that complexify cultural theory in the light of the habit of dualism. We claim that the immanent philosophies of DeLanda and Braidotti (though by no means exclusively), in their early as well as their recent incarnations, exemplify the constitution and enactment of new materialist cultural theory.

This chapter engages with the constitution of new materialism, as an object of study and a shared ambition with the scholars whose work we study. Following the interviews in Part One of this book, and building on a comprehensive review of enactments or instantiations of new materialism in recent cultural theory, this chapter proposes that the immanent gesture of new materialism is transversal rather than dualist as it intersects academic (neo-)disciplines (for instance feminist theory, science and technology studies, and media and cultural studies), paradigms (for instance the Saussurian/Lacanian linguisticism that is still prevalent in cultural theory today, or the dualistic take on the natural sciences and the humanities), and the linear spatiotemporalities conventionally assigned to epistemic trends (for instance "new" materialism versus Marxist historical materialism as practiced by Benjamin for instance[4]). Our proposition is that new materialism is itself a distinctive trend, both in feminist theory and in cultural theory more broadly, and a device or tool for opening up theory formation. This is to say that new materialism not only allows for *addressing* the conventional epistemic tendency to what can be summarized as classification or *territorialization* (when a new trend appears on the academic stage, it is usually interpreted as a "class" that can be added to an existing classification of epistemologies), but also—and at the same time—for *de-territorializing* the academic territories, tribes, and temporalities traditionally considered central to scholarship. After all, the classificatory strategy perfectly exemplifies transcendentalism and the two characteristics of dualism (sequential negation and a narrative of progress). Braidotti has summarized the need for this double move as a "qualitative leap" towards "creating conditions for the implementation of transversality" (ibid., 123). In this chapter, we intend to affirm the *transversality* of new materialism. That is to say, we study and propose a new materialism that *cuts across* or intersects dual oppositions in an immanent way. Félix Guattari ([1964] 1984), coining this term as early as 1964, insists on the "micropolitical" nature of transversality, introducing it as a means to search for the new—not by critiquing the old, but by radically questioning (or smoothening out) all the barriers that supported its logic. "Transversality is the transference become vehicular" as Gary Genosko (1996, 15) then concludes. The strength of new materialism is precisely this nomadic traversing of the territories of science *and* the humanities, performing the agential or *non-innocent* nature of all matter[5] that seems to have escaped *both* modernist (positivist) and postmodernist humanist epistemologies.

New Materialism Generated: Depending on Disciplines

Although we want to show here that a first instantiation of transversality enacted by new materialist cultural theorists cuts across scholarly disciplines, there is a whole range of scholars working on new materialism from their respective disciplinary locations. In these specific disciplinary takes on new materialism, the potentialities of the new materialism get lost in unnecessarily narrow understandings. Introducing new materialism *into* a discipline entails a transcendental gesture according to which the new materialism and the discipline in question (e.g. sociology) are positioned as pre-existing or *generated* rather than generative, and consequently as interacting rather than intra-acting. In other words, due to the presumed schism or dualism, the transversality of new materialism is being undone rather than affirmed or put to work. To transversalize can only be done when always already "invoking a new frame of analysis," as Jonathan Gil Harris (2003, 281) puts it. A new materialism that emerges *from* a discipline is an immanent gesture that we will discuss in the next section.

Momin Rahman and Anne Witz (2003, 245) in "What Really Matters? The Elusive Quality of the Material in Feminist Thought," for instance, focus exclusively on sociologically induced feminisms, and argue that "there needs to be a recognition of both the limits of a constructionism grounded in materialism and the potential of a constructionism that deploys materiality as a more porous and flexible concept." Rahman and Witz recognize the shift engendered by a new materialism (conceptualizing "materiality"), and claim that the conceptualization of the material employed in the early days of feminist sociology was more complex than simply economical. This cartography is in line with what we want to present here. Although new materialism has set in motion a *qualitative shift* in cultural theory at large, this shift is transversal, not dualist. Striking alliances between the old and the new, Rahman and Witz claim that early feminists broadened the definition of the economically determinist material to include social relations and the domestic sphere, and worked on the material as including everyday and institutional practices as well (ibid., 250). As a consequence, they read Butler's claim about "the distinction between the material and the cultural [being] no longer a stable or viable one" (ibid., 249) as an outrage, precisely because of the fact that 1970s and 1980s feminist sociology did not necessarily work along the lines of such a distinction. In the work of Butler, they imply, a second-wave feminist materialism functions as a straw person.[6] Rahman and Witz find that good-old feminist sociological work worked along the lines of an expanded conceptualization of the material.

Simultaneously, however, they claim that the good-old feminist sociological work simply *added* new (relativist, they say) theoretical frameworks to the existing economically determinist materialism. They question whether, in such a context, "the distinctive materiality of materialism has any residual conceptual integrity" (ibid., 252). In other words, they stumble upon the problems of additive/quantitative epistemic approaches, especially, we would say, when the two quantified approaches are non-exhaustive oppositions. We claim that adding a so-called feminist postmodern epistemology with relativist inclinations to a modern epistemology, feminist or not, materialist or not, does not necessarily result in a qualitative shifting of *either* the modern *or* the feminist postmodern. This is why the questioning of conceptual integrity is justified in the case of the cartography of Rahman and Witz, but not in the context of new (feminist) materialism per se. The conceptualization of "materiality" that the sociologists Rahman and Witz engage with does not necessarily shift the term towards something that differs from the economical simply because of the fact that early feminist sociologists seem to have *added* a bodily materiality *to* the economical.

The materialism brought to the fore by Rahman and Witz—if compared with economical (neo-classical) materialism, the constructionist approach remains constant, as DeLanda also stressed in the interview in Part One—should in fact be labeled "new" in the teleological sense of the term, whereas we have argued that it is among other things *teleology* (as shared by realist/totalizing/modern and social constructivist/relativist/ postmodern epistemologies) that is broken down in new materialism. Rahman and Witz themselves yearn for a breakdown of linear continuity as well, while remaining in a dualistic mode (pre-distinguishing the social and the physical), which we would interpret as an artifact of their territorial approach to new theory formation:

> The social constructionism being worked at here is not one that is limited by physical matter, but rather one that is able to incorporate body matters as an indivisible part of lived, gendered experience and action. [...] it seems to us that there is an attempt to consider the *social* effectivity of the physical—materiality as embodiment, experienced and rendered meaningful within gendered and sexualized frameworks of meaning and action (ibid., 256; original emphasis).

Rahman and Witz thus affirm dualisms throughout their article—the dualism between new materialism and sociology being the starting point, and the one between physicality and sociality being the end result. It seems as if they have wanted to rescue (good-old) feminist sociology in light of a materialism that is new in the teleological sense of the term.[7] Analyzing their article, we have shown that such an approach does not allow for the qualitative shifting of concepts that is to be found in the work of, among others, Braidotti and DeLanda. The materiality celebrated remains reduced to being the polar opposite of a sociality—that is, the material here has to be made socially effective, rather than seeing the social and the material as co-constitutive forces through, for instance, the "abstract machine." We read this absence as an artifact of the authors buying into disciplinary territoriality. Bringing new materialism (here assumed to be a pre-existing body of work) into contact with a scholarly discipline (equally assumed to be pre-existing) has distortive effects. The presupposition that a new materialism is *generated* contradicts new materialism's own *anti-representationalism*. New materialism, then, takes scholarship into absolute deterritorialization, and is not an epistemic class that has a clear referent. New materialism is something to be *put to work*.[8]

Cultural theory being less disciplined than (feminist) sociology, the beginnings of a *transversal* understanding of new materialism can be found in Susan Sheridan's "Words and Things: Some Feminist Debates on Culture and Materialism." Sheridan (2002, 23), while not using the term new materialism herself, argues that the impact of post-structuralism on feminist cultural theory has resulted in the displacement of "the primacy of social and economic relations in analyses of women's situation," and in the implementation of taking into consideration the primacy of "issues of sexuality, subjectivity and textuality." Sheridan claims that this seeming shift rests on a misinterpretation of post-structuralist theory, in which words and things got separated (all of a sudden "words" gained primacy) whereas post-structuralism, if read unpolemically, and together with recent work on matter, "demonstrates how inseparable are the symbolic and the material in examining the discursive construction of 'objects' of knowledge, and the material effects of that discursive power" (ibid., 25). In other words, post-structuralism and new materialism in Sheridan's understanding should not be read as dual opposites, and together they should not be seen as theoretical moves *beyond* a feminist sociological materialism. This cartography is qualitatively different from the one presented by Rahman and Witz, and it finds confirmation in the work of French post-structuralist feminists such as Hélène Cixous ([1975] 1976, 879, 884), one of whose main concerns, after all, was representationalism.

Sheridan, like Braidotti, positions herself amongst post-structuralist feminists who have argued that cultural constructivist feminism "is not materialist enough" (ibid., 27), and who have attacked "reductive (essentialist) representations of the nature/culture binary divide itself" (ibid., 28). Here, a post-structuralist feminist cultural theory seems to be dualistically opposed to a "cultural constructivism." Post-structuralist feminists are said to have critiqued cultural constructivism for working with a "de-materialised body," whereas another critique is that they have been working with "understandings of 'discourse'" that are "limited" when language is taken to be performative (ibid.). At the same time, post-structuralist feminist cultural theory is said to have attacked the reductive essentialism of *both* feminist sociology (focusing on the material) *and* cultural constructivism (focusing on the cultural). Traversing the non-exhaustive opposites of feminist sociology and cultural constructivism, and analyzing the reductivism effected on the basis of a reliance on *either* matter *or* discourse demonstrates transversality. In other words, Sheridan argues that the current rise in new materialist analyses in cultural theory shows that *both* language-oriented cultural constructivisms *and* sociologically induced feminisms are to be critiqued, since *neither* has fully employed the agential qualities of matter. Sheridan's reading of what she calls a "new stage" (ibid.; cf. Hekman 2010, 7 on a "new settlement") in feminist theory generates a focus not only on biological matter or on a cultural theory incorporating insights from the natural sciences, but also on the matter of the political economy, thus qualitatively shifting a concept of matter as purely physical and opposed to the social or linguistic.

The new stage's disciplinary transversality comes to be fully delineated by Stacy Alaimo and Susan Hekman (2008, 9–10; cf. Squier and Littlefield 2004) as a new materialism (here called "material feminism") that is to be found in the disciplines of "science studies, environmental feminisms, corporeal feminisms, queer theory, disability studies, theories of race and ethnicity, environmental justice, (post-)Marxist feminism, globalization studies, and cultural studies," and which as an epistemic trend is involved in "integrating them into what amounts to a new paradigm for feminist thought. [...] this paradigm is currently emerging and [...] is a necessary and exhilarating move for contemporary feminism." In *The Material of Knowledge: Feminist Disclosures*, Hekman (2010) goes so far as to demonstrate that new materialism is to be found in *all* scholarly disciplines, cutting across the trans-Atlantic disconnection between analytic and continental philosophy, and putting feminist theory at the forefront. For us, too, the new materialism allows for a move away from disciplines towards the meta-disciplinary, in feminist theory and in cultural theory more broadly, which is a claim that alludes to the importance of studying and engaging with the effect that this move might have on the *paradigms* of contemporary cultural theory. In what ways does new materialism traverse paradigms?

Generating New Materialism: Playing with Paradigms

Demonstrating the workings of new materialism, that is, generating a new materialism rather than relying upon a new materialism already pre-generated, Braidotti (2000, 160) argues that what is to be found in postmodern cultural theory (i.e. the body of social/semiotic constructivist cultural theory considered state-of-the-art once theory formation is positioned on a global classificatory map) is a "denial of the materiality of the bodily self" in paradoxical conjunction with the fast circulation of an excessive number of theoretical discourses about, and cultural representations of, the human body. In other words, cultural theory in the postmodern era has been unable to account fully for materiality, whereas it found itself surrounded by an excessive representation (thus objectification) of (bodily and non-bodily, organic and inorganic, always already feminized) matter in popular culture as well as cultural theory. Braidotti takes postmodernist constructivism's specific form of anti-essentialism, which affirms representationalism, to be responsible for this curious situation. Postmodernist constructivism is discovered to be a paradigm in which the space for materialism is, in Alistair Welchman's words (2005, 390), "restricted," and postmodern cultural theorists are simply included in the huge category of "critics who use an impoverished conception of matter inherited from non-materialist systems of thought" (ibid., 388). Postmodern cultural theory, otherwise seen as constituting and having been constituted by the *Crisis* of Reason, seems to have continued to work within the legacy of modernism's foundationalism. The modernist system of thought relying on Reason (and concepts like Logos, Mind, Representation) has not been fully broken down, and this is why transcendental and humanist tendencies continue to haunt present-day cultural theory. We have already explained that a postmodernism dualistically opposing modernism cannot entail anything but a continuation of the Same (cf. Alaimo and Hekman 2008, 2–3, Hekman 2010, 48). How does new materialism succeed in qualitatively shifting the paradigm that had supposedly already left the academic stage after May '68? And how does it introduce a conception of matter that is *not* impoverished?

As already stated, Braidotti's new materialism, which she also terms a "bodily" or "carnal" materialism (2006, 182) begins with "the enfleshed Deleuzean subject," which is "a folding-in of external influences and a simultaneous unfolding outwards of affects." The exterior and the interior, the subject(ive) and the object(ive), the individual, the social, and the symbolic are conceptualized as co-constitutive instead of pre-determined levels or layers. The genealogy of this Deleuzean subject is created in Continental thought; it includes "Descartes' nightmare, Spinoza's hope,

Nietzsche's complaint, Freud's obsession, Lacan's favorite fantasy, Marx's omission" (Braidotti 2000, 159). This cartography shows that new materialism has something to say about Reason/the modernist paradigm as well as the Crisis of Reason/the postmodernist paradigm. In other words, it is a *qualified* cartography, which opens up for a qualitative shifting of a dual opposition. This shifting is done by rethinking matter. Affirming a radical sense of materialism, or simply radical immanence, instead of starting from Reason (whether adjectified, thus postmodernized, or not), Braidotti does not define matter as solid and stable, as self-identical. A radically immanent conceptualization of matter *necessarily* affirms its ongoing "metamorphosis" (Braidotti 2002a), or in the words of DeLanda (1996, 2002), its ongoing "morphogenesis" as it shows an interest in intensive material processes and the actual forms they can produce.

According to a philosophy of radical immanence informed by a Bergsonian concept of time (*durée* instead of linearity and progress), matter is not thought of as Matter, the photonegative of Reason or Logos or Mind or Representation, but rather by a focus on "duration [inserted] into matter" (Grosz 2005, 111). It is a focus, indeed, on metamorphosis or morphogenesis:

> What endures, what is fundamentally immersed in time is not what remains unchanging or the same over time, a Platonic essence, but what diverges and transforms itself with the passage of time (ibid., 110).

This boils down to matter *immanently escaping* every possible representation in the modernist, scientistic meaning as well as in the postmodernist, social or semiotic constructivist sense of the term according to which representation is not the scientific "mirror of nature" but rather the equally representationalist "mirror of culture" (Barad 2007). This is to say that whereas a modernist scientific materialism allows for one, True representation of matter, and a postmodernist cultural constructivism allows for a plethora of equally true representations, it is the *shared representationalism* that is questioned and shifted by new materialism. Matter is a transformative force *in itself*, which, in its ongoing change, will not allow any representation to take root. This is also how Miguel de Beistegui (2004,

110) reads Deleuze with Heidegger, elusively concluding that: "Behind or, better said perhaps, beneath every object, every representation, every physical of metaphysical ideality lies a phenomenon, which is the flesh and blood of the world, the life that continues to live in and through being as it is represented in itself. This is being as it is *lived*."[9]

In "What is the Matter of Feminist Criticism?" Mariam Fraser affirms Braidotti's new materialism, by working on the academic whom Claire Colebrook (2004, 293) has called the epitome of contemporary (feminist) postmodern cultural theory: Judith Butler. Representationalism or linguisticality is key to the work of Butler.[10] Fraser (2002, 613) claims that in this work, language ends up addressing only the exterior. As a corollary, the interior appears as fundamentally ungraspable as any grasping is done through language. How do Barad and Vicki Kirby, whom Fraser positions alongside Braidotti for the generation of new materialism, qualitatively shift the relation between matter/materiality and language, between the exterior and the interior of the body? The key point is the abandonment of assumptions about linguisticality, and about who does the speaking/writing. For Barad (1998, 105 in ibid., 618; original emphasis), "what is being described by our theories is not nature itself, but our participation *within* nature." She theorizes the intra-action of the observer, the observed, and observing instruments, all of which are "agential." In line with this, Kirby starts from the literacy of matter, re-reading Derrida and Saussure in order to show that a close reading of their work also uncovers their emphasis on materiality-in-change. In the work of Kirby, matter appears as something that is not only spoken about or spoken with, but rather as itself simply *speaking*. Nature and culture, word and flesh are "all emergent *within* a force field of differentiations that has no exteriority in any final sense" (Kirby 1997, 126–7 in Fraser 2002, 619; original emphasis). Both cases of transversality, signified by the "within," entail leaving behind the primacy of either language/culture or matter/nature. In other words, a false dualism comes to be traversed. New materialism, that is, cuts across postmodernist and modernist paradigms as it shows that *both* epistemologies start from a distinctive pole of what Colebrook (2004, 56) has called "the representation/materiality dichotomy." Questioning this dichotomy involved the following:

When feminists criticized or rejected the notion of women as mired in material embodiment, they did so because matter was deemed to be devoid of dynamism. When, subsequently, that phobia regarding matter was questioned, it was precisely because the border between mind and matter was deemed to be the effect of a prior linguistic or social production. And when 'linguisticism,' in turn, was challenged, this was because language had been erroneously taken to be a fixed, determining, and inhuman grid imposed upon life, rather than a living force (Colebrook 2008, 64).

Bodies are texts that *unfold* according to genetic encoding, Braidotti says, which implies traversing the material and the representational.

Key to the new materialist paradigm, then, is an emphasis on the "material-discursive" or "material-semiotic" that we know from the paradigm-shifting work of Haraway (1988, 595; original emphasis):

> [...] bodies as objects of knowledge are material-semiotic generative nodes. Their *boundaries* materialize in social interaction. Boundaries are drawn by mapping practices; 'objects' do not pre-exist as such. Objects are boundary projects. But boundaries shift from within; boundaries are very tricky. What boundaries provisionally contain remains generative, productive of meanings and bodies. Siting (sighting) boundaries is a risky practice.

Such a claim is transversal when it comes to the broad (modernist and postmodernist) paradigms of cultural theory. The focus on the *materialization* of bodies and other so-called objects of investigation demonstrates how "duration" has in fact gotten "inserted into matter" (how DeLanda, for instance, got to focus on "matter-energy flows"), and how the "the representation/materiality dichotomy" has indeed been broken down (how Braidotti, for example, came to conceptualize the body as "a piece of meat activated by electric waves of desire, a text written by the unfolding of genetic encoding") in new materialist cultural theory. Working with "material-semiotic agents," as Haraway calls them, allows for a complexification of the way in which matter used to be defined. An object is no longer passive matter that has to be re-presented; meaning-making takes place on a two-way track.¹¹ Here it is also demonstrated how new materialism does not discard signification (cf. Ahmed 2008, 34) but rather directs it to its proper place and qualitatively shifts the linguistic turn accordingly (i.e. non-dualistically).

In the passage cited above as well as in her later work, Haraway focuses upon the ways in which bodies and systems of scholarly signification/representation materialize alongside each other. Harawayian instantiations of new materialism affirm what Barad (2007) has called an onto-epistemology, or even an ethico-onto-epistemology, according to which being and knowing (and the good) become indistinguishable. Inspired by Haraway and Barad, we lastly wish to discuss the *cartographical methodology* that generates and is generated by the disciplinary and paradigmatic transversalities of new materialism.

Cartography Rather Than Classification

New materialism is a cultural theory for the twenty-first century that attempts to show how postmodern cultural theory, even while claiming otherwise, has made use of a conceptualization of "post-" that is dualistic. Postmodern cultural theory re-confirmed modern cultural theory, thus allowing transcendental and humanist traditions to haunt cultural theory after the Crisis of Reason. New materialist cultural theory shifts (post-)modern cultural theory, and provides an immanent answer to transcendental humanism. It is a cultural theory that is non-foundationalist yet non-relativist. In conformity with the interviewees in Part One of this book, we have shown that there is much to be gained from an argument such as the latter; after all, postmodernisms and modernisms are manifold, on the one hand, and epistemologically very similar on the other. It is for this reason that new materialism continues to rewrite the history of philosophy. As already stated, the minor tradition Deleuze proposed is now widely read and commented upon, but increasingly, great minds of the past are being given the attention that their work needs. For there is no need to limit this tradition to a series of personae or even to what the History of Philosophy has labeled a particular "type" of thinking. Scholars at work within modernism such as Bergson, Whitehead, William James and Edmund

Husserl, all of whom had been pushed aside or reinterpreted by dualist thinking, are in need of serious materialist re-readings, which are in fact being carried out by an increasing number of scholars today. There is not even any reason to exclude Hegel from this list. For when he stated that "Action divides [spirit] into substance and consciousness of the substance" (Hegel [1807] 1977, paragraph 444), this not only comes very close to Spinoza's solution to the mind-body problem with which this chapter began, it also allows us to rethink Marx's (Hegel-inspired) materialism as a (non-dualist) neo-materialism. The richness of all these philosophies had by and large been suffering from dualism-dominated modernism and postmodernism. The way in which new materialism was generated in the previous paragraph alluded to the fact that duration not only came to be inserted into matter (ontology), but also and simultaneously into theory formation (epistemology). In other words, theory formation also entails the materialization of boundaries. Starting theory formation from *movement* alludes to cartography rather than classification, which is the third instantiation of transversality that we intend to highlight in this chapter.

In the introduction we claimed that new materialism not only *enacts* a thinking about theory formation that is other than classificatory (new materialism sets in motion a non-dualistic epistemic practice), but also that it enables us to understand the way in which theory formation used to be thought (following a territorialization pattern). We claimed that classification exemplifies the territorial and is fully dualistic, and throughout this chapter we have made clear how seemingly opposite epistemic tendencies or classes are in fact non-exhaustive oppositions. New materialism criticizes not only the use of "a discipline" or "a paradigm" as pre-determined, but is also critical, along the lines of the dismantling of binary oppositions that it enacts of the pre-determination of classifications of theoretical trends. Classifying epistemic tendencies that are supposedly prevalent in cultural theory implies working along territorial lines, which is a transcendentalizing gesture along with invoking sequential negation and a narrative of progress (i.e., it is dualist). This does not allow for the (un)folding of cultural theory—the matter-energy flows of theory formation, the non-linear coding practices, the cutting across matter and signification—to be captured. New materialism de-territorializes the ways in which cultural theory has been classified, and this process we call cartographical. We referred above to Colebrook, who questioned a conceptualization of "language" as "a fixed, determining, and inhuman grid imposed upon life." She defined new materialism as allowing us to see not only matter, but also language as a "living force." Questioning fixity thus opens up the possibility of thinking about theory formation in a non-linear, cartographical way.

Barad's "Re(con)figuring Space, Time, and Matter" is useful for explaining the move away from the classificatory towards the cartographical. Earlier we mentioned Barad's neologism "intra-action," which allowed us to demonstrate that terms such as mind and matter, or sociology and new materialism, do not exist independently before they begin to inter-act. Barad (2001, 98) explains the machinery of intra-action as follows:

> [...] structures are to be understood as material-discursive phenomena that are iteratively (re)produced through ongoing material-discursive intra-actions. This machine is not a Euclidean device, nor is it merely a static instrument with a non-Euclidean geometry. It is a topological animal which mutates through a dynamics of intra-activity. Questions of connectivity, boundary formation, and exclusion (topological concerns) must supplement and inform concerns about positionality and location (too often figured in geometrical terms).

Affirming onto-epistemology, Barad talks about mapping practices that draw boundaries, and she claims that *the same* objects/boundaries materialize in non-exhaustively opposite mapping practices (Euclidean space versus stasis in non-Euclidean space). The mapping practice, generating intra-action and generated through it, shifts both options and works along the following lines:

> What we need are genealogies of the material-discursive apparatuses of production which take account of the intra-active topological dynamics that reconfigure the spacetime manifold. In particular, it is important that they include an analysis of the connectivity of phenomena at different scales. [...] The topological dynamics of space, time, and matter are an agential matter and as such require an ethics of knowing

and being: Intra-actions have the potential to do more than participate in the constitution of the geometries of power, they open up possibilities for changes in its topology, and as such interventions in the manifold possibilities made available reconfigure both that will be possible. The space of possibilities does not represent a fixed event horizon within which the social location of knowers can be mapped, nor a homogenous fixed uniform container of choices. Rather the dynamics of the spacetime manifold is produced by agential interventions made possible in its very re(con)figuration (ibid., 103–4).

These genealogies, or "cartographies" in our vocabulary, are non-dualist approaches to theory formation that allow for absolute deterritorializing. Not primarily interested in representation, signification, and disciplinarity, new materialism is fascinated by affect, force, and movement as it travels in all directions. It searches not for the objectivity of things in themselves but for an objectivity of actualization and realization. It searches for how matter comes into agential realism, how matter is materialized in it. It is interested in speeds and slownesses, in how the event unfolds according to the in-between, according to intra-action. New materialism argues that we know nothing of the (social) body until we know what it can do. It agrees with studying the multiplicity of modes that travel natureculture as the perpetual flow it has always already been.

In the next chapter we will take up the question of non-dualism, and we will discuss in a detailed manner *how* new materialism pushes dualism into non-dualism, thus allowing for a non-reductive take on matter and language.

Notes

1. This mapping of new materialism overlaps considerably with the one produced by Myra J. Hird (2004, 2006), albeit that we (much like Barad in the interview earlier in this book) do not argue that new materialism has gotten off the ground in the natural sciences, and that there are varieties of feminist *applications* of new materialism. We will demonstrate in this book how new materialism traverses both the sciences and the humanities *necessarily*, and how it is immediately a feminism.
2. For this term see Barad 2007.
3. We take this formulation from Grosz 2005.

4. For an interesting take on Benjamin's take on historical materialism, see Tiedemann 2005, 157–63.

5. See Dolphijn 2004, 24.

6. See van der Tuin 2009 for a conceptualization of "second-" and "third-wave feminist epistemologies."

7. See van der Tuin 2008 and Davis 2009 for a critique of a biologically tainted argument about new materialism (namely Ahmed 2008). A comparison between Sara Ahmed's work and Rahman and Witz will show that, whether sociologically or biologically biased, a disciplinary take on the new materialism is always already a reduction. New materialism proposes to study the biological and the sociological as intra-acting, thus as relating, rather than as two independent relata that might *inter*act.

8. Despite the most original and radical thoughts by which DeLanda has inspired so many scholars *and* scientists all over the world, a returning critique on his work has to be that the scholarly areas of his interest never even seem to connect to one another. Whether it concerns his revolutionary take on geology, biology, sociology, architecture, mathematics or historiography (which only seem to be some of the fields of which he has proven himself to be an expert), the disciplinary boundaries, contrary to the way Deleuze and a lot of other scholars working with Deleuze today deal with this, stay firmly in tact.

9. It is necessary, for an affirmative reading of Heidegger, that we do not consider his conceptualization of "being" as opposed to a (for instance Whiteheadian) becoming, as Shaviro (2009, ix) proposes. This is very possible if we commit ourselves to a different reading of the former's texts. For when, in conceptualizing "being," Heidegger ([1980] 1994, 66) states: "Hegel brings the absolute restlessness of absolvence into this quiet 'is' of the general proposition," he affirms that "being" equals this "true immediacy" which allows us to understand being as equal to metamorphosis or morphogenetic change. Beistegui's "phenomenon" provides further proof for new materialism's (as yet underresearched) relation with (new) phenomenology.

10. Although it is undeniable that Butler features as the epitome of linguisticism in new materialist theory formation, new materialist theorists also try to read her affirmatively. Kirby's *Judith Butler: Live Theory* from 2006 is an excellent example hereof, since one reads the attempt to push Butler beyond linguisticism, and thereby towards new materialism, between the lines on every page. Kirby (2006, 162, n. 2; original emphasis) states that "[...] contributions to the *question* of matter are compatible with Butler's political project, even through they radically extend its terms." Butler herself often feeds the dualism between new feminist materialism and linguisticist feminist theory. In her recent work *Frames of War: When is Life Grievable?* for instance, Butler (2009, 30) distances herself explicitly from Spinozist currents that are so influential, above all, in contemporary Australian feminist (materialist) theory (*cf.* Kirby 2006, 150 *ff*). Also when she (Butler) claims that the body reveals itself to us in and according to language (she uses the term "the interstices of language" ([1987] 1999, 193) it makes it easy to conclude that indeed this is a linguisticism at work.

11. Instantiations are to be found in the work of among others Gallagher (2005) and Massumi (2002).

Chapter 6
Pushing Dualism to an Extreme

This chapter engages with the way in which several significant contemporary (Continental) philosophers establish a philosophy of difference in the form of a "new materialism." It builds on work on new materialism's specific philosophical impetus as well as carefully unpacking the methodology through which it is actualized. Though we will demonstrate that this double move concerning ontology on the one hand and methodology on the other is inherent in the new materialism, most contemporary commentaries focus on ontology only by *positing* the new philosophical stance. In other words, the materialism of new materialism is reflected upon, whereas a clear perspective on how new materialism is *new* remains underdeveloped. This chapter addresses this discrepancy by demonstrating how the new materialism produces a revolution in thought by traversing modernity's dualisms (structured by a negative relation between terms), and by constituting a new conceptualization of difference (structured by an affirmative relation) along the way. This conceptualization of difference entails an ontological philosophical practice predicated on leaving behind all prioritizations (implicitly) involved in modern dualistic thinking, since a difference structured by affirmation does not work with predetermined relations (e.g. between mind and body) nor does it involve a counter-hierarchy between terms (which would make the new materialism into a postmodern philosophical exercise).

The "new" of new materialism (that is, the way in which its non-dualist philosophy is related to dualist philosophical stances) comes close to Jean-François Lyotard's plea for a "rewriting" of "modernity." In chapter 2 of his *The Inhuman* ([1988] 1991) Lyotard, who is famous for his thoughts on "post-modernism," critiques this concept in particular because of its implicit notion of time. Postmodernism *is* modernism in the sense that the issues raised by modernism are also on the agenda of postmodernism, which is rather an after-modernism. Issues, as Lyotard continually stresses, that predominantly include the emancipation of humanity as a whole. Yet by appropriating the term post-modernism, his project automatically claims itself to be a linear consequence of modernism *and* (at the same time) refuses to think the here and now (or at least, it can only think the here and now as a consequence of a period in cultural history long gone). In re-reading Aristotle's *Physics* (Book IV), however, Lyotard agrees with the idea that what has already taken place (*proteron*) and what is about to take place (*husteron*) cannot be considered apart from the now. Both history and the future unfold from the now. Our age then should not be considered an age that follows from modernity, but rather an age that sets itself to a continuous rewriting of several of the (emancipatory) features that have been raised by modernity, thus actively creating a past (while projecting a future). That is why Lyotard ([1988] 1991, 24) suggests rephrasing his project as "rewriting modernity."

The idea of rewriting modernity might also be considered a good description of what Gilles Deleuze (Lyotard's close colleague at the University of Vincennes) proposed. Deleuze (e.g. [1966] 1991) too seems to accept the Aristotelian notion of time, which, in his books, is mainly at work in how Henri Bergson rewrote Aristotle (using the concepts of actuality and virtuality). Deleuze himself (like his interpreters) always claimed that he intended to rewrite the history of philosophy as a whole, or at least, his goal—especially in the early part of his career—was to question the History of Philosophy (with capital letters) as a whole, as its dominant lines of thought overcoded many ideas that he considered to be of the greatest value. Yet without prejudice to his timeless contributions to thought, there are good reasons to consider the work of Deleuze not so much a rewriting of the entire History of Philosophy, but rather as a rewriting of modernity.

For although authors like Lucretius, Duns Scotus, and the Stoics play an important role in his thinking, they have never been at the centre of a particular study, nor has Deleuze made much effort to shed new light on their ideas. He did, however, give philosophy and many other parts of academia important rewritings of philosophers such as Spinoza, Leibniz, Nietzsche and Bergson, and writers like Proust and Kafka. These were authors who, in very different ways, all lived their lives in the so-called modern era. Renaming Deleuze's project as "rewriting modernity" seems all the more agreeable, because its key feature, being the emancipation of humanity in its most radical form, seems *precisely* what Deleuze's philosophy is all about. Gilles Deleuze's (and Félix Guattari's) rewriting of modernity was about the rewriting of a "minor tradition" in thought, as it was named (e.g. Deleuze and Guattari [1980] 1987), which is mainly based on the four "modernist" thinkers mentioned above. By rewriting their modernity, and not in the least place modernist ways of thinking emancipation, Deleuze did not create a post-modernism that continued (in any way) the traits that had given form to the modern era. Rather, in line with how Lyotard conceptualized it, Deleuze's goal was to set this whole tradition in movement. We will show later that Deleuze's take on the Other, for instance, cannot be captured by the post-modern countering of the One.

In Lyotard's wake, the perpetual rewriting of modernity is something also taken very seriously by those inspired by new materialist thought today, as already seen in the interviews in Part One of this book and subsequently noted at the end of the previous chapter. The work of this rapidly growing group of contemporary scholars rewrites modernism, or bits of modernism, opening this (philosophical) tradition up to the arts and the sciences, actualizing and realizing it in the here and now. Some authors, like Braidotti and DeLanda, are very much interested in re-reading Deleuze and his minor tradition, though it should be mentioned that both of them are also using other fertile (modern) grounds. Braidotti has always shown an interest in psychoanalysis (Freudian psychoanalysis in particular). DeLanda, on the other hand, though always viewed as a committed Deleuzian, makes at least as much use of the work of Fernand Braudel, Mario Bunge, and Max Weber. Others, like Karen Barad and Quentin Meillassoux, have come to this path through still other routes. Barad (2007), emerging from the field of theoretical physics, is mostly inspired by the work of Niels Bohr. Quentin Meillassoux ([2006] 2008) sets himself to rewriting the dominant stream in the modernist project as a whole (which he labels "correlationalist"), which brings him back most of all to an affirmative re-reading of David Hume.

All of these authors are in touch with a material spirit whose imperceptible forces they perform in their writing in diverse ways. Yet their common interest in doing this *affirmatively*, in and through a re-reading of modernity, demands more refinement. For instance, in *Nomadic Subjects* Braidotti (1994, 171), in a Lyotardian vein and in reference to Deleuze's minor tradition, states that we ought to "work through" the notion of woman: "Like the gradual peeling off of old skins, the achievement of change has to be earned by careful working through; it is the metabolic consumption of the old that can engender the new." Expanding their interest in "naturecultures" (as Donna Haraway [2003] puts it) or in "collectives" (which is a concept of Bruno Latour ([1991] 1993)), the way in which they rewrite modernity's processes is by rewriting the dualisms that are so central to modern thought. Latour for instance has stated that he is "trying the tricky move of unveiling the modern Constitution without resorting to the modern type of debunking" due to the fact that his project is to affirm "that the [modern] Constitution, if it is to be effective, has to be aware of what it allows" (Latour [1991] 1993, 43). This kind of argumentation can be summarized, in the words of Bergson ([1896] 2004, 236), as a movement of "push[ing] dualism to an extreme." In this chapter we discuss the way in which a new materialism comes to be constituted precisely by this movement, which Deleuze ([1956/2002] 2004, 32) in discussing Bergson has typified as methodological (it touches upon ways of arguing, ways of doing philosophy) as well as ontological (it is interested in a material spirit, that is, in what Brian Massumi [2002, 66] calls "ontologically prior"). It is the type of movement Deleuze himself has adopted as his own methodology, especially in *Capitalism and Schizophrenia*, the diptych written together with Guattari. In their *Anti-Oedipus* ([1972] 1983), they already claimed to perform what they called a "schizoanalysis" (a materialist philosophical practice interested in conceptualizing sexuality beyond the male/female dualism and even beyond human sexuality), and in breaking through the Oedipal plot that overcodes the ways in which we think (through psychoanalysis), and oftentimes individually and collectively experience, desire. Far from respecting Cartesian dualisms, this style of thinking is much more interested in rethinking Spinoza's monist solution by means of these oppositions and what they can do, as Eugene Holland argues (1999, 111–2). But it was in *A Thousand Plateaus* (Deleuze and Guattari [1980] 1987, 20) that they came closest to capturing their project in words, when they state as follows: "We invoke one dualism only to challenge another. We employ a dualism of models only in order to arrive at a process that challenges all models." Hence, the methodology and ontology proposed in rewriting modernity in no way "follows from" modernity. By pushing dualism to an extreme, "difference is pushed to the limit" (Deleuze [1968] 1994, 45). Consequently, by radically rewriting the dualisms of modernity, new materialism precisely becomes a philosophy of difference that opens up for a "new" ontology, or rather, a "new" ontogenesis.

In the previous chapter we suggested that new materialism is a transversal cultural theory that qualitatively shifts the dualist gesture of prioritizing mind over matter, soul over body, and culture over nature that can be found in modernist as well as post-modernist cultural theories. We thus "invoke[d] the same testimony" (Bergson [1896] 2004, 236) against two seemingly opposite cultural theories. Despite the fact that such prioritization appears commonsensical even today in prominent parts of the sciences and the humanities, its reliance on dualism is by no means beyond question. The outcomes of the prioritization exercises are generally presented as True in its most totalizing meaning, whereas minor traditions throughout the centuries have opposed them in convincing ways. In other words: a new materialism is constituted by demonstrating how the canonized relations between the aforementioned terms are in fact the outcomes of "power/knowledge" according to which Truth is an instantiation of a politics or régime, as Michel Foucault (1980) would have it. In this chapter we will take our previous arguments a step further by focusing on the methodological and ontological issues surrounding the present-day rise of non-dualist thought. We will begin by considering what a radical rewriting of modernity in the case of new materialism entails. *How* do scholars such as Braidotti, DeLanda, Barad, and Meillassoux produce their work?

New Materialism's Radical Rewriting of Modernity

Let us agree on the point that a cultural theory can only be truly distinctive and *original* if its establishment does not claim to be the next step in a discussion that is structured according to the dominant lines of sequential negation and the narrative of progress; that is, if its installment does not follow the classificatory lines that started dominating thought within modernism as it has branched off into so many different parts of life. Similarly, *opposing* this narrative is also not an option. Lyotard has already taught us that his increasing concern with the idea of postmodernism also had to do with the prefix "post-," and the way this opposed yet (re)created the narratives of modernity. As already mentioned in the previous chapter, it was Michel Serres who put the latter into a general theory, when he stated: "An idea opposed to another idea is always the same idea, albeit affected by the negative sign. The more you oppose one another, the more you remain in the same framework of thought" (Serres with Latour 1995, 81).

Therefore, not just the idea of postmodernism but actually *all thought* that starts either with classification or with the repudiation of it, does not radically rewrite, cannot set forth a revolution in thought. Elizabeth Grosz (2005, 165), who follows Luce Irigaray's investment in thinking through (feminist) revolutions in thought, states most clearly that it is *only* in a radical rewriting that revolutions in thought can come into being. After all, such movement

> is not a revolution on any known model, for it cannot be the overthrow of all previous thought, the radical disconnection from the concepts and language of the past: a revolution in thought can only use the language and the concepts that presently exist or have already existed, and can only produce itself against the background and history of the present.

Earlier, Grosz (2000) had already explained that the seemingly constraining model, or framework of thought, or concept allows in fact for the indeterminacy of a revolution in thought.[1] Wishing to anticipate future thoughts and practices by negating the past, one positions oneself in a relation to past thoughts and practices that is solely constraining. In such a situation, the past undergoes nothing but re-confirmation in the present, albeit that progress is assumed to be made. *This*, we want to argue, is the structuring principle of classificatory modes of thinking, which are consequently prevented from a radical rewriting of thought, from being truly revolutionary.

Our goal in this chapter should thus be to find out in what way the revolutionary constitution of new materialist cultural theory rewrites modernity as a present according to which a past and future unfold. In order to get there we shall first demonstrate by what means the new materialist breakdown of dualism, of the structuring principle of modernist cultural theories, stirs a revolution in thought. New materialist cultural theorists do not involve themselves with ongoing repetitive discussions in the modernist humanities (cf. Serres with Latour 1995, 86). New materialism helps us analyze and (therefore) shift the structuring principles of these discussions by showing how classificatory negation involves a specific relationality, which is reductive. Later we will demonstrate how new materialist cultural theories are not relational in a negative, reductive manner, but rather are structured along the lines of an affirmative intensity, which in the end turns into a non-dualism, a monist philosophy of difference, or more precisely, *immanence*. Invoking one dualism in order to challenge another allows new materialism to rewrite modernity *as an* emancipation.

Dualism: A Negation is a Relation Structured by Negativity

Bergson ([1869] 2004, 297) argued that "[t]he difficulties of ordinary dualism come, not from the distinction of the two terms, but from the impossibility of seeing how the one is grafted upon the other." Bergson's "ordinary dualism" indicates the structuring principle of Serres' repetitive discussions, and Grosz's (failed) overthrow of previous thought. Even in our time cultural theory is structured predominantly according to this ordinary dualism. It continues—implicitly or explicitly—the modernist framework of thought, accepting and thinking along the dominant lines of dualist distinctions of mind and matter, soul and body, and culture and nature. But although Bergson demonstrated that ordinary dualism is inherently problematic, the act of making distinctions between terms is not. The treatment the distinguished terms receive is what makes dominant cultural theory, then as now, questionable. Bergson implies that as long as we are clear about the fact that one term of a dichotomy is "grafted upon" the other, we will not fall into the trap of setting up a discussion that leads us away from serious thought. This also applies to how contemporary thought, often through denial, is grafted upon modernist cultural theory—such as through Barad's term "representationalism," as will be discussed below.

Let us provide an example that proves our point. Consider a big name in contemporary sociology and philosophy: Jean Baudrillard. Baudrillard was no doubt part of a very talented generation of French scholars that also included Lyotard and Deleuze. But in contrast with the latter two, Baudrillard was from the outset very much accepted in mainstream cultural theory. He is the prototype of those post-modernist thinkers from whom Lyotard implicitly wanted to distance himself, insofar as Baudrillard wholeheartedly accepts the modernist dualisms and continues their arguments. There is no other way to think, for instance, of Baudrillard's theory of simulacra (e.g. Baudrillard [1981] 1995, [1995] 1996) as anything other than a continuation of modernity, as a general acceptance of its theories, and a refusal actually to rewrite the dualisms involved. Discussing for example the imaginary of Disneyland, he concluded that "[i]t is no longer a question of a false representation of reality (ideology) but of concealing the fact that the real is no longer real, and thus of saving the reality principle" (Baudrillard [1981] 1995, 12–3), he refuses to make any analysis whatsoever of the duality of real vs. representational. Accepting the difference (even while twisting it around) is by no means the way in which new materialism is always already questioning these principles and rewriting them from the start.

Thus the time has come to draw a formal difference between this ordinary dualism, as Bergson analyzes it, and the radical writing of modernist dualisms as proposed by Lyotard and Deleuze, but also by scholars such as Latour. The difference lies not in the fact that this latter group suggests a dualism that begins with the act of relating whereas ordinary dualism denies this relational nature. Rather, both groups start from this relating (insofar as it exists outside of its terms). Yet ordinary dualism is undergirded by a *negative* relationality, and it is this particular type of relationality that is not subscribed to by Lyotard, Deleuze, or Latour (or even Bergson, for that matter). Let us continue therefore by focusing more specifically upon the set-up of argumentations about the deficiency of ordinary dualism. We have to return once more to Bergson, whose work provides insight into the ways in which the concrete cases of ordinary dualism that structure cultural theory (the humanities) as well as scientism and common sense can be overcome. Yet his work also shows how non-dualist philosophy is always "onto-epistemological" (Barad's term)—that is, how philosophy involves the way in which "concept and creation are related to each other" (Deleuze and Guattari [1991] 1994, 11). This refers back to Deleuze's remark about the work of Bergson as both methodological and ontological: Bergson not only provides insight into ordinary dualism as the structuring principle of non-revolutionary thought, but also he re-writes modernism so as to provide a non-dualist ontology structured by the "unity of the thing and the concept" (Deleuze [1956/2002] 2004, 33).

When Bergson introduces the concept of ordinary dualism in *Matter and Memory*, he works on the problem of the union of body and soul. The centrality of this union comes to the fore, according to Bergson ([1896] 2004, 235), on the basis of a distinction made between matter and spirit. This ontological distinction, and more importantly the specific way in which it is treated, constitutes Bergson's analysis as exemplary of the (necessary) circumvention of ordinary dualism. Moreover, a distinction is still being made between terms:

> We maintain, as against materialism, that perception overflows the cerebral state; but we have endeavoured to establish, as against idealism, that matter goes in every direction beyond our representation of it [...] And against these two doctrines we invoke the same testimony, that of consciousness, which shows us our body as one image among others and our understanding as a certain faculty of dissociating, of distinguishing, of opposing logically, but not of creating or of constructing. Thus, [...] it would seem that, after having exacerbated the conflicts raised by ordinary dualism, we have closed all the avenues of escape [...] But, just because we have pushed dualism to an extreme, our analysis has perhaps dissociated its contradictory elements (ibid., 236; cf. Balibar [1989] 1998, 106 on Spinoza).

This lengthy quotation provides insight into the way in which the terms that are divided up by ordinary dualism are grafted upon one another, but also in the way in which ontology and methodology/epistemology are grafted onto one another. The two levels of analysis (for lack of a better term) indicated here are intrinsically intertwined. We want to underline that "all the avenues of escape" do exactly not end up being "closed," because of the complexity with which Bergson shifts ordinary dualism and moves into the direction of thinking differently, of thinking a non-dualist ontology. Let us explain this complex move by seeking recourse to Deleuze and Guattari's *What is Philosophy?*, this time read through the work of Barad.

Deleuze and Guattari ([1991] 1994, 11) state that "the question of philosophy is the singular point where concept and creation are related to each other." *Not* defining the nature of philosophy as such would seduce one into uncritically affirming commonsensical and scientistic representationalism, found also in the humanities, which is predicated upon an ordinary dualism in a two-leveled manner. Barad (though without referring to Deleuze and Guattari) elaborates upon precisely this point. In "Posthumanist Performativity: Toward an Understanding of How Matter Comes to Matter" she states:

> The idea that beings exist as individuals with inherent attributes, anterior to their representation, is a metaphysical presupposition that underlies the belief in political, linguistic, and epistemological forms of representationalism. [...] representationalism is the belief in the ontological distinction between representations and that which they purport to represent [...] (Barad 2003, 804).

In other words: what she calls for is a "performative understanding, which shifts the focus from linguistic representations to discursive practices" (ibid., 807).[2] We have alluded to these practices already, when we explained how philosophy both addresses and explains the structuring principles of the dominant, classificatory lines of thought. The work of Barad can explain that what Bergson ([1896] 2004, 260) calls thinking through scientism, or common sense, or the one pole of any dualism (in the humanities too) "in its remotest aspirations," one affirms an onto-epistemology. According to onto-epistemologies, "[w]e do not obtain knowledge by standing outside of the world; we know because "we" are *of* the world. We are part of the world in its differential becoming" (Barad 2003, 829; original emphasis). Onto-epistemology demonstrates how philosophers do philosophy, which following Deleuze and Guattari ([1991] 1994, 11) is a discursive practice according to which

> the concept is not given, it is created; it is to be created. It is not formed but posits itself in itself—it is a self-positing […] The concept posits itself to the same extent that it is created. What depends on a free creative activity is also that which, independently and necessarily, posits itself in itself: the most subjective will be the most objective.

Philosophers do philosophy in their work with concepts, when studying the concepts that arise in a specific practice and which are related to concepts that are at work in other practices with which they interfere. Elsewhere, Deleuze clearly states that when it comes to what philosophy does, he will not accept that it is any form of representational dualism structured by negative relationality. The created concepts, he claims, are no less "practical, effective or existent" (Deleuze [1985] 2000, 280) than the practices in which they happen. Thus "philosophical theory is itself a practice just as much as its object. It is no more abstract than its object" (ibid.). Doing philosophy, then, means engaging in this creation of concepts, and not relying on "referential signs" (our term).[3] The latter is a representationalism, implying a negative relationality that does not do justice to matter as "the aggregate of images" and perception of matter as "these same images referred to the eventual action of one particular image, my body" (Bergson [1986] 2004, 8; original emphasis).

When Bergson ([1896] 2004, 243) invokes "consciousness" against materialism and idealism, and against empiricism and dogmatism, he claims that this concept can show that "a third course lay open," which allows him to escape from the representationalist traps affirmed in any dualist philosophy. His conceptualization of consciousness, which shows in this case how the four epistemic classes are all predicated on ordinary dualism on the two levels of analysis simultaneously, breaks through ordinary dualisms by positing a continuity against discontinuity, that is, a "pure duration" (ibid., 243). Such a concept cuts across metaphysical classes, that is, it creates a third, and revolutionary course:

> Homogenous space and homogenous time are then neither properties of things [materialism, realism] nor essential conditions of our faculty of knowing them [idealism, dogmatism]: they express, in an abstract form, the double work of solidification and of division which we effect on the moving continuity of the real in order to obtain there a fulcrum for our action, in order to fix within it starting-points for our operation, in short, to introduce into it real changes. They are the diagrammatic design of our eventual action upon matter (ibid., 280).

The third course, then, opens the way for "the true power of creation" (ibid., 236), which we already encountered in the work of Deleuze and Guattari, and will find in the work of de Beauvoir as well. This power is not attributed to *either* body *or* mind, *either* matter *or* the perception/representation of matter, or any other such alternative. The creation of concepts entails the breakdown of representationalism on two levels. This revolutionary shifting entails precisely the activity of "pushing dualism to an extreme," which opens the way for a thinking in action that is affirmative, practical and thus necessarily revolutionary.[4]

Difference, or: The Shift to Affirmative Relationality

Pushing dualism to an extreme helps to further our thoughts about new materialist cultural theories and the way in which they are constituted. New materialism does not rely upon a representationalism; it shifts the representationalist metaphysical premises of Bergson's ordinary dualism by invoking a discursive practice centered on the creation of concepts *in their relationality*. The often binary oppositions that dominated modernity, and that are still accepted as premises in much of the theory of our age (which can therefore be considered post-modern, as Lyotard defined it) are structured by a relation of negations, and by re-affirming these negations. New materialists instead install a philosophy of difference by engaging in the activity of creating concepts, which is an onto-epistemological activity. A relationality in the negative, dualistic sense presupposes the terms of the relation in question, whereas the creation of concepts entails a *traversing* of dualisms, and the establishment of a relationality that is affirmative—i.e., structured by positivity rather than negativity. What happens here is that "difference is pushed to the limit" (Deleuze [1968] 1994, 45). By "pushing dualism to an extreme," "difference is pushed to the limit," the latter movement being less evaluative and more performative. Let us now demonstrate the workings of the affirmative relationality and the philosophy of difference thus constituted.

In *A Thousand Plateaus*, Deleuze and Guattari ([1980] 1987, 20–1) state that they "[a]rrive at the magic formula we all seek—PLURALISM = MONISM—via all the dualisms that are the enemy, an entirely necessary enemy, the furniture we are forever rearranging." Similar to Bergson, Deleuze and Guattari do not avoid or negate dualisms, but traverse or pass through them. This affirmative approach to the modern, ordinary dualisms is an instance of what Lyotard called a rewriting of modernity. It shows how dualisms are inherently untenable, whereas holding on to a negative relationality between terms appears historically to be seductive. (Even feminists have fallen into the trap of relying too much on such a dualist logic!) Bergson and Deleuze and Guattari effectuate an *affirmative* take on the way in which two terms relate, and this shifts dualism by pushing it to an extreme. In an affirmative approach, a dualism does not only involve a binary opposition, a relation structured by negativity according to which different-from is necessarily worth-less-than (Braidotti 1994, 147).[5] The starting point is that "[r]elated terms belong to one another" (Deleuze [1968] 1994, 30). Only when this sense of belonging is affirmed are we able to work "towards an absolute concept, once liberated from the condition which made difference an entirely relative maximum" (ibid., 33). It is precisely the activity of working towards an absolute concept that defines the rewriting, the revolution in thought that interests us.

Deleuze contends in *Difference and Repetition* that "The negative and negativity do not even capture the phenomenon of difference, only the phantom or the epiphenomenon" ([1968] 1994, 52). This phantom-like character of negation should be taken literally, because here Deleuze produces a critique of representationalism. Capturing difference can only be done when "difference" is "shown *differing*" (ibid., 56; original emphasis) when the thinking does not start with the respective phenomena that are then claimed to be different from one another, but with mapping *difference in itself*. How does this work? In "Postmodernism is a Humanism: Deleuze and Equivocity," Claire Colebrook (2004, 287) asserts that "one should go beyond the fantasy and structure of signification to its possibility." What we are looking at here is the invention of the conditions of invention (cf. Serres with Latour 1995, 86)—namely, the establishment of a non-dualist logic of univocity as opposed to the dualist logic of equivocity: whereas "equivocity posits two radically incommensurable levels" (that which signifies, e.g. gender, and that which is signified, e.g. sex/the body), "there is just one plane of expression" according to a static univocal logic (Colebrook 2004, 288). Colebrook goes on by stating that "*both* the simple image—as a world of simulation, signification, representation or social construction—*and* the criticism of this notion are equivocal without justification,"[6] whereas under a univocal logic "truth may be intuited as that which expresses itself, not as that which is in itself and then belied by relations, but that which gives birth to—while remaining irreducible to—relations" (ibid., 290; original emphasis. Cf. Bleeker 2008). Under univocal logic, "a perception of x is perceived as a power *to x*" (Colebrook 2004, 297; original emphasis) which is to say that difference is shown *differing*. Here we see an affirmation that feminism as a practice has nothing to offer but paradoxes: it posits sexual difference and is emancipatory insofar as the hierarchical element (different-from as worth-less-than) is broken down. Equivocity, that is, is locked up in a dualist framework of thought, structured by negativity (and linear time: sexual difference implies that women/femininity should become equal to men/humanity), whereas univocity pushes difference to the limit, producing a shift to an affirmative relationality (producing a situation in which, as we will see that de Beauvoir envisioned, new and as-yet inconceivable carnal and affective relations between the sexes are born). By way of another example: in the concluding section of "Postmodernism is a Humanism" Colebrook talks about the work of Virginia Woolf who pushes equivocal gender to univocal sexual difference, thus evoking a situation in which "[t]here are no longer distinct kinds or generalities, or genders, so much as essences that are the power to differ, essences that are sexual precisely because they have their sole being in creation" (ibid., 304; cf. below).

The remaining question is *how* exactly differing or affirmative relationality is a non-dualist univocity? Deleuze demonstrates how representationalism is an identity politics or régime in what he calls the major History of Philosophy (with capitals). In case difference is thought of in terms of identity (under this dominant way of thinking, assuming one perspective or multiple perspectives), the Other (e.g. the woman), a concept so central in the work of other early philosophies of difference (think of Levinas and Derrida, for instance), can only be thought to exist in relation to the One, or Same, or Centre. Rejecting the idea that otherness can be reduced to a particular subject or object, thus refuting the idea that his philosophy starts with an *ontology* of the One (as Alain Badiou [1999] wrongly supposes), Deleuze ([1969] 1990, 307) then concludes that "the Other is initially a structure of the perceptual field, without which the entire field could not function as it does. [...] It is the structure of the possible. [...] The terrified countenance bears no resemblance to the terrifying thing. It implicates it, it envelopes it as something else, in a kind of torsion which situates what is expressed in the expressing." This is when and where a dualism comes to be installed that is structured by negativity (distribution), and when and where different-from is transformed into worth-less-than (hierarchy or asymmetry). It is for that reason that Deleuze himself, contrary to his contemporaries, found it difficult to relate this concept to his thoughts. The Other is the expression of a possible world as he, reading Tournier's *Friday*, developed this idea in *Difference and Repetition*. In an interview with *Magazine Littéraire* (reprinted in Deleuze [1988] 1995, 135–155) and in a letter he wrote to his Japanese translator Kuniichi Uno (reprinted in Deleuze 2006, 201–203) he continued this argument by making an implicit comment on Derrida's "Letter to a Japanese Friend" ([1985] 1988) and his use of the Other as Deleuze comes up with a Japanese man whose words can function as the expression of a possible world. Contrary to Derrida (referring to Heidegger [1959] 1971) who emphasizes the non-translatability of his French text into Japanese and yet simultaneously the necessity to do so, Deleuze does not accept the relative existence of the One (the Same, the Centre) and the Other (here the

French language and the Japanese language) and the negative relation drawn between them. In line with the anti-correlationism of Meillassoux, Deleuze ([1988] 1995, 147) stresses that the expression of a possible world (even when done in Japanese), "confers reality on the possible world as such, the reality of the possible as something possible [...]."

In contrast to the negative dualism then, and in line with the Bergsonian virtual/actual pair, Deleuze proposes a logic according to which "[e]ach point of view must itself be the object, or the object must belong to the point of view." (Deleuze [1968] 1994, 56; cf. Leibniz [1714] 1962, 263 §57, Deleuze [1956/2002] 2004, 39) That is to say, the moment we think *differing* or *difference in itself* a univocal logic is established. This occurs when we think dualism to an extreme—Deleuze states that it is *within* Kantianism, or "*in the same stroke*" (Deleuze [1968] 1994, 58; original emphasis) that such a shift is effectuated. Difference is then established as "the element, the ultimate unity," that is, difference that "refer[s] to other differences which never identify it but rather differentiate it" (ibid., 56). Difference then comes awfully close to the (mathematical) object that speculative realists and materialists like Graham Harman and Meillassoux talk about. Meillassoux's statement that "[t]here is no reason for anything to be or to remain self-identical" (Meillassoux [2006] 2008, 88) emphasizes this difference in itself, this difference always already differing. Refusing the idea that "to be is to be in a correlate," (as Harman [2011b, 15] summarizes Meillassoux's critique of correlationist ontology), Deleuze states that difference is not in need of relations yet at the same time does not exist in a void. It is a thinking according to which

> [e]ach difference passes through all the others; it must "will" itself or find itself through all the others. [...] a world of differences implicated one in the other, [...] a complicated, properly chaotic world *without identity* (Deleuze [1968] 1994, 57; original emphasis).

Referring to the work of Nietzsche, Deleuze states that

> What is then revealed is being, which is said of differences which are neither in substance nor in a subject: so many subterranean affirmations. [...] for a brief moment we enter into

that schizophrenia in principle which characterises the highest power of thought, and opens Being directly on to difference, despite all the mediations, all the reconciliations, of the concept (ibid., 58).

In other words: what is established is the univocal logic (ibid., 67).

It should not come as a surprise that it is not only Nietzsche who then practices philosophy as a creative act, but Bergson as well. In "Bergson's Conception of Difference," Deleuze ([1956/2002] 2004, 33; original emphasis) states that "either philosophy proposes for itself *this* means (differences of nature) and *this* end (to arrive at internal difference)" or else it would always end up in a representationalist, equivocal logic. Bergsonism, as said, is looking for "the unity of the thing and the concept," that is, for a philosophy that practices a univocal logic. Such a logic enacts what we previously called an onto-epistemology whose concept of difference is predicated on affirmation. Deleuze is explicit about this when he says that Bergson "rais[es] difference up to the absolute" (ibid., 39) by thinking difference following a univocal logic, which entails a qualitative shift away from equivocity, that is, among other things, negation:

> If duration differs from itself, that from which it differs is still duration in a certain sense. It is not a question of dividing duration in the same way we divided what is composite: duration is simple, indivisible, pure. The simple is not divided, *it differentiates itself.* This is the essence of the simple, or the movement of difference. So, the composite divides into two tendencies, one of which is the indivisible, but the indivisible differentiates itself into two tendencies, the other of which is the principle of the divisible (ibid.; original emphasis).

The relational nature of the structuring logic is kept in place (previously we saw that Bergson continues to make distinctions). But relationality at work is not predicated on equivocal notions such as negation, or analogy for that matter, because the relationality is never predeterminable from the outside. Deleuze ([1956/2002] 2004, 40, 42) even explicates how "vital difference" for Bergson is "not a determination" but rather "indetermination itself," which is not to say that it is "accidental" but rather that it is "essential." In other words, "[d]ifferentiation is the movement of a virtuality actualizing itself." This non-reductive, univocal take on difference cannot be a dialectic and cannot be structured according to dualism, because according to Bergson

> the negation of one real term by the other is only the positive actualization of a virtuality that contains both terms at once. [...] The opposition of two terms is only the actualization of a virtuality that contained them both: this is tantamount to saying that difference is more profound than negation or contradiction (ibid., 42–3).

Allowing for the virtual, for pure recollection, to be reflected in the actual, constantly exchanging the two into one another as it creates the circuit of duration—this is what Bergsonism does. Such a philosophy, which amounts to a new materialist rewriting of modernity, is the production of revolutions in thought *not* by negating ordinary dualism (the structuring principle or equivocal logic of modernist thought), but rather by pushing ordinary dualism to the extreme, thus installing a new take on difference, the univocal logic of which is an affirmative relationality. Such a philosophy is the activity of pushing difference to the limit by traversing dualism.

When speculative realists and speculative materialists today propose to move away from Kantian correlationism to the "eternal-in-itself, whose being is indifferent to whether or not it is thought" (Meillassoux [2006] 2008, 63), they push dualism to the extreme in a similar way. When Harman (2010, 202) for instance notes a "[...] global dualism between the reality of objects and their more or less distorted or translated versions for other objects," he follows Bergson's distinction between difference in itself and ordinary difference. The latter is representationalist and negative, while the former demonstrates an interest in the true power of creation (Bergson), morphogenesis (DeLanda), or metamorphosis (Braidotti).

New Feminist Materialism Pushes Sexual Difference to the Limit

Let us close with a provocative example of a rewriting of modernity, which will be developed further in the next chapter. Previously we hinted at the possibility of transforming equivocal gender—which is structured by a negative relationality (distribution and asymmetry) between men and women, masculinity and femininity—into univocal sexual difference, which allows sexual difference to *differ*. New feminist materialism is the cultural theory that enacts this possibility. New feminist materialist cultural theorists work along the lines of affirmative relationality, the workings of which we have demonstrated in the previous section. In doing so, they push sexual difference to the limit by pushing the dualism that is ordinarily installed (gender) to an extreme. The new feminist materialism does practical philosophy and thus produces a revolution in (feminist) thought. In this final section we will address new feminist materialist cultural theory, not only because it can demonstrate the workings of difference structured by a univocal logic of affirmative relationality, but also because feminism per se is an interesting site for our exposé about new mater-ialist cultural theory, that starts with difference *as a practice*, that is not "about" sexuality or gender (as a theory opposed to the practice or act) but that is a practice or act itself, by means of the concepts it gives rise to and through which it practices its power.

Feminism has always enveloped sexual difference in its ordinary dualist sense as well as the traversing thereof. Both movements were a necessity for feminism, as Joan Wallach Scott (1996, 3–4; original emphasis) explains:

> Feminism was a protest against women's political exclusion; its goal was to eliminate "sexual difference" in politics, but it had to make its claim on behalf of "women" (who were discursively produced through "sexual difference"). To the extent that it acted for "women," feminism produced the "sexual difference" it sought to eliminate. This paradox—the need both to accept *and* to refuse "sexual difference"—was the constitutive condition of feminism as a political movement throughout its long history.

The book in which Scott makes this complex diagnosis is entitled *Only Paradoxes to Offer*, and we want to demonstrate here why the situation she explores is in fact not at all paradoxical. Sue Thornham (2000, 188; original emphasis) makes exactly this point, when she explores the work of Irigaray:

> One cannot, she writes, analyse the gendered nature of culture by stepping out of the identity "woman" into a gender-neutral discourse—by claiming an "equal right" to speak—because there *is* no gender-neutral discourse; the public discourse of analysis is thoroughly masculine. To write from outside that discourse is, however, to be ignored. To do either is to remain within the terms of the dominant discourse.

Despite the fact that many feminists, including Irigaray and Braidotti and Grosz and Colebrook, have found their individual and/or generational answer to the seeming paradox, we want to show here how feminism *is* Scott's diagnosis, which is not a paradox that is in need of a solution.

Grosz (2005, 156), a feminist new materialist, states that major Philosophy, a philosophy structured by the dominant lines of thought, has traditionally excluded women, whereas it has produced a discourse that is implicitly gendered masculine. Philosophy has objectified women, thus erecting the male philosopher figure. The Irigarayian analysis of this ontoepistemological diagnosis proceeds as follows:

> The question of sexual difference signals the virtual framework of the future. What today is actual is sexual opposition or binarism, the defining of the two sexes in terms of the characteristics of one. Sexual difference is that which is virtual; it is the potential of this opposition to function otherwise, to function without negation, to function as full positivity. It is the future we may be able to make, but which has not yet come into existence (ibid., 164).

That is to say, sexual difference functions prominently in feminist theory: namely, both as an ordinary dualism and as virtuality. Feminist theory will produce a revolution in dualist thought not by overcoming sexual difference (conceptualizing emancipation as a striving for equal gender relations or as the overthrow of a discourse that is gendered masculine) but by traversing it (allowing for sexual *differing*). Feminist theory has to push sexual difference as an ordinary dualism to an extreme precisely so as to push sexual difference to the limit. A sexual difference according to which women are worth-less-than men, to speak with Braidotti, has to be pushed to an extreme so as to release sexual difference as that which is virtual. This is precisely how we should read Simone de Beauvoir's conclusion to *The Second Sex*, which indeed thinks through the emancipation of humanity in its most radical form. After a full description of the dialectic of sex (a dualism structured by a negative relationality), she concludes that: "new carnal and affective relations of which we cannot conceive will be born between the sexes" (de Beauvoir [1949] 2010, 765). It is precisely by thinking through sexual difference to its remotest aspirations, thus alluding to difference structured by an affirmative relationality, that de Beauvoir came to produce the revolution in thought that has made her famous (and infamous), for constituting feminism as a rewriting of modernity—that is, feminism-as-differing. de Beauvoir exemplifies a new materialist take on difference, since by traversing the (sexual) dualism structuring modernist thought, modernity comes to be rewritten and difference is shown *differing*.

Notes

1. The feminist point being that women are not "to deny [...] the resources of prevailing knowledges as a mode of critique of those knowledges" (Grosz 2005, 165). When modernity can be (re)thought as thinking emancipation, women had better affirm it.

2. Deleuze and Guattari ([1980] 1987, 66) use the concept of "discourse" similarly to how Barad does. Following Foucault, this long quote brilliantly explains how this does away with the linguistic representations that have been so important in academia up until today:

   > Let us follow Foucault in his exemplary analysis, which, though it seems not to be, is eminently concerned with linguistics. Take a thing like the prison: the prison is a form, the 'prison-form'; it is a form of content on a stratum and is related to other forms of content (schools, barracks, hospital, factory). This thing or form does not refer back to the word "prison," but to entirely different words and concepts, such as 'delinquent' and 'delinquency', which express a new way of classifying, stating, translating and even committing criminal acts. 'Delinquency' is the form of expression in reciprocal presupposition with the form of content 'prison.' Delinquency is in no way a signifier, even a juridical signifier, the signified would be that of the prison. That would flatten the entire analysis.

3. Grosz (2005, 123) reminds us of Maurice Merleau-Ponty's criticism of precisely the onto-epistemological aspect of the work of Bergson. He claims that it is a transcendentalism. We, however, do not define the onto-epistemological as "collapsing our knowledge of a thing with its being" and accept another onto-epistemology.

4. In an article that questions the monism of Bergson and claims that his work is Eurocentric and phallocentric, Rebecca Hill (2008, 132–3) ends with the following conclusion, thus undoing the argument presented in the article, yet affirming consciousness as a concept:

In my view these passages demonstrate the valorization of a hypermasculine theory of life and corresponding devaluation of matter as feminine. This is not a binary hierarchy because Bergson's concepts of life and matter are never actualised as pure activity and pure space. [...] matter's inclination towards pure repetition is never fully achieved. [...] At the same time, life is not manifested as pure creative energy. [...] Moreover, Bergson admits that if materiality was pure repetition, consciousness could never have installed itself within matter's palpitations.

5. When different-from translates into worth-less-than, emancipation either means the inclusion of women, laborers, black people, and other Others in the hierarchically privileged domain (a strategy of equality) or the revaluation of the underprivileged domain (a strategy of difference). This binary opposition will be repositioned in the final section of this chapter.

6. In other words: modern and post-modern cultural theories are both structured along the lines of an equivocal logic.

Chapter 7
Sexual Differing

Feminist historiography writes histories of feminist thought as well as providing a specific definition of feminism. As such, "feminism" is not only reflected upon by feminist historiographers; feminism is also *created* in feminist historiography. We already saw how in *Only Paradoxes to Offer: French Feminists and the Rights of Man*, Joan Wallach Scott (1996, 3–4; original emphasis) specifies how "sexual difference," in turn, structures and is structured by feminism:

> Feminism was a protest against women's political exclusion; its goal was to eliminate "sexual difference" in politics, but it had to make its claim on behalf of "women" (who were discursively produced through "sexual difference"). To the extent that it acted for "women," feminism produced the "sexual difference" it sought to eliminate. This paradox—the need both to accept *and* to refuse "sexual difference"—was the constitutive condition of feminism as a political movement throughout its long history.

Sexual difference, then, serves two purposes at the same time, which (as Olympe de Gouges already remarked) is the cause of a sense of paradox: on the one hand, "exclusion was legitimated by reference to the different biologies of women and men," whereas on the other hand, "'sexual difference' was established not only as a natural fact, but also as an ontological basis for social and political differentiation." (ibid., 3) This diagnosis implies a diversified and unusual ontology of sexual difference, an ontology not made explicit in the major historiographical tradition in gender studies. Its major tradition all too often involves the need to choose between (biological) essentialism and social constructivism as well as a *critique* of patriarchal politics, which does not allow feminism or gender studies to move beyond a merely reactionary stance. As we will show below, a critical stance re-affirms what is critiqued. A *radical* feminism does not allow itself to exist as encapsulated by the political mainstream. When feminism is constructed as *inherently* paradoxical, however, one's ontological condition as a woman/female feminist is not seen as predetermined by either biology or social construction (whether this is a strategic essentialism or a diversification of the category of "women"). Rather, (biological) essentialism and social constructivism are two discourses that feminism traverses, which implies a performative understanding of ontology. In other words, the category of woman materializes through the traversing of non-feminist and feminist discourses that make sexual differentiations. Here, feminism's opposition to biological determinism, translating into a social constructivism as of the dominant Anglo-American reception of Simone de Beauvoir's seminal work *The Second Sex*, is shifted by allowing for "natural facts" or "sex" to have a place on the conceptual map, the leaving behind of biological *predetermination* notwithstanding. Such mappings of relations between the sexes do not seem to allow for nature and culture to be disentangled. An ontology that we have specified as "performative" implies diverting from the major tradition in feminist historiography (a tradition predicated on dualism structured by negation) and "reading for the historically specific paradoxes that feminist subjects embody, enact, and expose" (ibid., 16).

Unconfined by the parameters of the dominant feminist historiography, Scott's analysis can be specified as an instantiation of Jean-François Lyotard's "rewriting modernity." Commenting on a teleological conception of the history of Marxism, Lyotard ([1988] 1991, 28) writes that whereas Karl Marx seems to have thought that by revealing the hidden source of "the unhappiness of modernity" humanity could reach full emancipation, the history of Marxism in fact shows nothing but the need for "opening the same wound again. The localization and diagnosis may change, but the same illness re-emerges in this rewriting." "[C]losure or resolution" (Scott 1996, 17) is not to be found on the horizon of (the history of) Marxism and feminism; all we find is a perpetual offering of historically specific paradoxes. These paradoxes, in the context of feminism, concern the false opposition between biological essentialism and social constructivism, a problem inherent to "the dualist logic of modernity" (Lyon 1999, 169). The double bind of biological essentialism and social constructivism shows how "biology" and ontology feature prominently in the history and historiography of feminism, or: have been dominating its discourses for a very long time. *Traversing* the poles of this dualism constitutes a minor tradition in feminist historiography that allows feminism to move beyond the intrinsically dualistic and reactionary stance we identified above. This tradition is minor, in the words of Gilles Deleuze and Félix Guattari ([1980] 1987, 105), when it is "different from that of the constant [...] by nature and regardless of number, in other words, a subsystem or an outsystem." A minor tradition never gets stuck as it always finds itself, like Scott's paradoxes, in creative movement (ibid.: 105–6). Exemplifications of this minor tradition in feminist historiography which work along these lines can be found in the so-called "French feminism" from the 1980s (think of Hélène Cixous, Julia Kristeva, and especially Luce Irigaray) and in today's new materialist writing as we see it at work in, for instance, Rosi Braidotti and Elizabeth Grosz.[1] This chapter seeks to hook onto this minor tradition, and to re-read the work of de Beauvoir along the lines that it sets out. This chapter, by presenting a new materialist case study on sexual difference, zooms in on the way in which new materialism, by way of its traversing of dualisms, is always already a feminism that is not identity political.

According to Grosz, the majority of feminist theories, or feminist historiographies, which are theories of the history of feminism, are teleological. As Grosz (2005, 162) claims:

> The future of feminism, on this understanding, is limited to the foreseeable and to contesting the recognized and the known. This limited temporality characterizes all feminist projects of equalization and inclusion as well as a number of projects within postmodern feminism.

The sense of paradox experienced by feminists is understood as a consequence of the teleological dialectics structuring the relation between the two feminist waves, and between feminism and patriarchy. An alternative position involves a historically specific, or *an-teleological* take on the history of feminism in which feminist subjectivity is seen as materializing, that is, in which the ontology of sexual difference is strictly performative. Whereas Scott is still in the process of opening up feminism to this new ontology by critiquing the major tradition in the historiography of feminist thought, Grosz seems to map a radically new materialism that has structural links to French feminism. Grosz indeed starts from "Irigaray, whose work on sexual difference has signaled the indeterminate, and possible indeterminable, necessity of feminist thought, a necessity which parallels or, in her terms, is isomorphic with, that of sexual difference, one of the incontestable and most inventive forms of biological and cultural existence" (ibid., 163). For Irigaray, feminism consists of the wish to restructure the relations through which the sexes are created as well as of the traversing of prevailing sexual differentiations on the personal, social, and symbolic level. These traversings, in addition, are always already at work in the practice of making sexual differentiations. Feminism as a restructuring and traversing exercise is in no way a dialectic, since all dialectics are prevented from affirming "the development of modes of action, thought, and language appropriate to and developed by both of the sexes" (ibid., 164). William James' radical empiricism already noted that any kind of position is necessarily preceded by a relationality thanks to which a position can be established. Along the same lines, while speaking about how gender, race, and sexual orientation also emerge and back-form their own realities, Brian Massumi (2002, 8) argues: "Passage precedes construction. But construction does effectively back-form its reality. Grids happen. So social and cultural determinations feed back into the process from which they arose. [...] To say that passage and indeterminacy 'come first' or 'are primary' is more a statement of ontological priority than the assertion of a time sequence."

Affirming such a development of traversing can engender what Irigaray calls a "revolution in thought," which does not imply "the overthrow of all previous thought, the radical disconnection from the concepts and language of the past," that is, a critique with reactionary consequences, but rather "a certain kind of insinuation of sexual difference back into those places where it has been elided, the insistence on the necessity that every practice, method, and knowledge can be undertaken in another way" (Grosz 2005, 165). Feminism is now seen as a "practical philosophy" that focuses on "the singular point where concept and creation are related to each other" (Deleuze and Guattari [1991] 1994, 11). The outcomes of such a practical philosophy remain unforeseen, because "[w]hat today is actual is sexual opposition or binarism, the defining of the two sexes in terms of the characteristics of one. Sexual difference is that which is virtual; it is the potential of this opposition to function otherwise, to function without negation, to function as full positivity" (Grosz 2005, 164). The practical philosophy it puts forward, then, is structured by a "performative understanding, which shifts the focus from linguistic representations to discursive practices" (Barad 2003, 807).

In this chapter, we try to further the development of sexual difference as a performative ontology. We call this "sexual differing": an allowance for sexual difference actually to *differ*. It involves a rewriting of sexual difference and sexuality not by means of dualist premises, but as a practical philosophy in which difference *in itself* comes to being. In a manner similar to how other important fields in contemporary cultural theory, circling around concepts like "race"/ethnicity, class, sexuality, and most recently age or generationality, are slowly crashing against the limits of critique, feminism too seems to get stuck within its emphasis on sexual difference as a social construction (gender) opposite to a biological essence (sex). Surrounded by a so-called post-feminist popular and academic imagery, gender studies scholars today find themselves paralyzed by the "paradoxes" that their pasts have offered on the basis of teleology, and dualism structured by negation. Earlier we argued for writing the modernist oppositions as a form of continuously rewriting them, and we can now add that there is no reason why feminism or gender studies should place themselves beyond or outside the dualist paradigms in which they have been circling for so long. Instead, the aim we set for ourselves is to find out in what way we are to develop a *different* feminism that sets itself to a radical and continuous rewriting of this opposition, postponing the epistemological finitude (to use Meillassoux's term) that it suggests. The feminism to come then works with sexual difference not as a paradox that needs to be solved, but rather as a virtuality, or as a discursive practice of sexual differing. Thus we set ourselves here to finding traces of sexual differing that can rewrite feminist theory, experimenting with the minor statements in the work of contemporary feminists, feminists of the past, and scholars who came from elsewhere but are equally engaged in the production of a performative ontology of sexual difference (e.g. Deleuze and Guattari, but also Rosi Braidotti and Karen Barad). For feminism to be indeterminate (infinite), not to be formed around *critique*, it has to allow for the provocation that practical philosophy offers sexual difference. This entails the affirmation of the fact that feminism *materializes* sexual difference described as paradoxical, and that feminism has to be understood precisely *as such*.

Despite the fact that the major tradition in feminist historiography features her work differently, we aim to show that the conclusion to *The Second Sex* neatly mirrors the Irigarayan undecidability affirmed by Grosz. We justify this claim by following Sara Heinämaa (1997, 33–4, n. 4) who has suggested that "we should reject the sex/gender distinction and Sartre's existentialism [which is also based on dualism structured by negation] as keys to de Beauvoir's texts" without, however, fully affirming Heinämaa's subsumption of the work under a Merleau-Pontian phenomenology instead.[2] Following a full description of sexual difference, de Beauvoir ([1949] 2010, 765) states that "new carnal and affective relations of which we cannot conceive will be born between the sexes." In other words, she finds that the asymmetries between the sexes are traversed while installed and maintained in patriarchy. Read as a practical philosophy, thus restructuring and traversing the gendered dualist logic of modernity, *The Second Sex* opens the way for the indeterminacy of sexual differing; right after the previous quote de Beauvoir claims that she "do[es] not see [...] that freedom has ever created uniformity" (ibid., 765). We will demonstrate in this chapter that opening up the dominant historiography of feminism by re-reading de Beauvoir has the potential to break through the multiple paralyses experienced by contemporary feminists. Along with that, the re-reading can offer us a way out of dualist thought per se that might be equally important to other minor streams of culture, that is, to those interested in searching for a meaningful alternative to how the concepts of "race"/ethnicity, class, sexuality and age have been equally paralyzed by this "binary" take on dualism. Rewriting feminist historiography thus builds up to a materialist rewriting of academia as a whole.

Neither Sex Nor Gender But Sexual Difference

The received view on de Beauvoir[3] is laid out in Judith Butler's "Sex and Gender in Simone de Beauvoir's Second Sex," which is a philosophical meditation on de Beauvoir's famous statement that "[o]ne is not born, but rather becomes, woman" (de Beauvoir [1949] 2010, 283). Butler (1986, 35) explains how de Beauvoir has disconnected sex and gender thus allowing for "a radical heteronomy of natural bodies and constructed genders with the consequence that 'being' female and 'being' a woman are two very different sorts of being." "Gender," then, "must be understood as a modality of taking on or realizing possibilities, a process of interpreting the body, giving it cultural form. In other words, to be a woman is to become a woman; it is not a matter of acquiescing to a fixed ontological status, in which case one could be born a woman, but, rather, an active process of appropriating, interpreting, and reinterpreting received cultural possibilities" (ibid., 36). This passage is important for its two implications that obviously structure Butler's own later work on the concept of gender (cf. Sönser Breen and Blümenfeld 2005).

First, Butler does not qualitatively shift ontology's assumed fixed status. In gender theory, natural bodies are implicitly ascribed to, albeit that the traditional assumption that sex defines gender is reversed. When gender defines sex, sex or bodily matter, however malleable, is still assumed to be passive. Butler (1986, 35) argues that "the female body is the arbitrary locus of the gender "woman," and there is no reason to preclude the possibility of that body becoming the locus of other constructions of gender." In Butler's reading of de Beauvoir, a strict dualism is installed, now articulated by gender as it refers to a form of expression, and sex as it refers to a form of content. The relation created between how both content and expression are formed is not relative but absolute. Extracting a signifier from the word (gender) and from the thing (sex), a signified in conformity with the word, subjected to the word, Butler restricts herself to an oversimplified idea of language which refuses to see how the politics active in sex and gender build upon a series of statements and states of things that have always already been intrinsically entwined with one another and that are always in processes of morphogenesis corresponding to one another. The ever-changing flows of matter and meaning would never allow themselves to be reduced to one signifier and one signified creating one sign. When Deleuze and Guattari ([1980] 1987, 67) speak of the "discursive multiplicities" of expression and the "nondiscursive multiplicities" of content they refer precisely to this infinite (not one-on-one) enfolding of matter and meaning, which has always already led to the "material-discursive," as Barad (following Donna Haraway) conceptualizes it. In terms of Butler's feminism, the (female) body is *not* understood to be performative, or, in Vicki Kirby's terms, "telling flesh" (Kirby 1997).

Second, and following from its fixed position as a signifier (of a signified), gender gets a fixed meaning too by suggesting that it is a modality of taking on or realizing possibilities. Grosz (2005, 106) has argued for the need to import the Bergsonian distinction between the conceptual pairs virtual/actual and possible/real in feminist theory, conceptual pairs that are defined as follows:

> The real creates an image of itself, which, by projecting itself back into the past, gives it the status of always-having-been-possible. The possible is ideally preexistent, an existence that precedes materialization. The possible, instead of being a reverse projection of the real, might be better understood in terms of the virtual, which has reality without being actual (ibid., 107).

Despite Butler's great hopes, conceptualizations along the lines of the possible/real limit biological or anatomical sex to the culturally foreseeable, recognized, and known (which is the equally limited "gender"). Grosz claims that "[t]o reduce the possible to a preexistent phantom-like real is to curtail the possibility of thinking the new, of thinking an open future, a future not bound to the present, just as the present is itself a production of the past" (ibid., 108). Butler's Lacanian re-reading of de Beauvoir, then, read along with Grosz, severely limits the potential of feminism to make a difference as its ontology and epistemology are confined by historically established gendered patterns, predicated on a linear and causal theory of time. Locating gender ultimately in the female body, that is, projecting the word into the thing like the present is projected back into the past, turns the future of feminism into a descriptive historicism, enslaved by a major History (Deleuze and Guattari's abovementioned "constant") according to which its paths are set out.

It is worth noting that Butler discusses ontology in de Beauvoir (and "women" in feminism; see Butler 1993, 187–222) in terms of *paradoxes*.[4] She states that for de Beauvoir "[w]e never experience or know ourselves as a body pure and simple, i.e. as our 'sex,' because we never know our sex outside of its expression of gender. Lived or experienced 'sex' is always already gendered. We become our genders, but we become them from a place which cannot be found and which, strictly speaking, cannot be said to exist" (Butler 1986, 39). Here we see that, indeed, sex is the Lacanian signified which needs to be coded by a (linguistic) signifier which is gender (only revealing itself temporarily and fragmentarily through metonyms and metaphors). Later on in the article, Butler states that "[n]ot only is gender no longer dictated by anatomy, but anatomy does not seem to pose any necessary limits to the possibilities of gender" (ibid., 45), thus ultimately affirming the body as fully malleable. The temporality underlying all of this is one according to which "gender is a contemporary way of organizing past and future cultural norms, a way of situating oneself with respect to those norms, an active style of living one's body in the world" (ibid., 40). This is where we find Grosz's observations confirmed: the past (sex) is constituted in the present (gender) and so is the future along the lines of a realization of possibilities. The possible in Butler's reading of de Beauvoir is a reverse projection of the real; we cannot know the possible outside of the real just as it has no active role in signification. The real, then, is sexual opposition or binarism indeed, which is projected back into the past. Flesh appears as mute; Butler's seeming revolution in thought vis-à-vis de Beauvoir is undone by the representationalism implied by the possible/real and the signifier/signified couplings (cf. Colebrook 2004). But how, then, should de Beauvoir be read so as to ascribe this Irigarayan undecidability, affirmed by Grosz, to the work?

In "de Beauvoir and Biology: A Second Look," Moira Gatens (2003, 274) clearly states that de Beauvoir's "point in *The Second Sex* is not that the natural body has no hold on social values or that it is 'value all the way down.'" Gatens reads de Beauvoir as affirming "an interactive loop between bodies and values" (ibid., 274) and gives two examples from *The Second Sex* of the entanglement of, rather than the unilinear causality between, sex and gender, one of which she discusses at length (the post-menopausal woman [ibid., 278–9]) and the other she mentions only in passing (women's eroticism [ibid., 273]). The post-menopausal woman, Gatens affirms, proposes an important challenge to the Butlerian grid laid over the work of de Beauvoir by allowing for the *bodies* (sex) of these self-identified *women* to influence their cultural interpretation, namely as *non-feminine* (gender). The body that is no longer menstruating is one of those examples that show how a body cannot be grasped with signifier/signified or possible/ real, as this sexed body refuses to conform to the word "gender" nor to a realization of sexual binarism. The same goes for women's eroticism, the other example Gatens comes up with. Like Gatens, Karen Vintges ([1992] 1996, 47) clearly states in *Philosophy as Passion: The Thinking of Simone de Beauvoir* that intersubjectivity, despite Jean-Paul Sartre debunking the notion, "comes about because both partners undergo a metamorphosis into flesh (*chair*) through emotional intoxication, and experience themselves and the other simultaneously as subjectivity and as passivity." In a slightly different register, then, making love allows for a "becoming 'flesh' [also: incarnation] through emotion" resulting in "a unification of body and consciousness" (ibid., 48). Vintges presents another convincing argument about de Beauvoir's anti-representationalism and her usage of the virtual/ actual coupling; the love-making de Beauvoir finds enabling is not modelled on certain modes (e.g. the Marquis de Sade's sadomasochism, or marital sex), and affects both sexes in unforeseeable ways (ibid., 48–9). Gatens (2003, 283) indeed states that the future, for de Beauvoir, is open and as yet unknowable to the mind (unfeelable by the body), due to her strong belief in truths as unfixed, as ambiguous, as inherently paradoxical. She affirms that "the incessant play between the two terms of a pair, say, nature and culture, is what constitutes our situation as always ambiguous, always involving a free 'becoming,' rather than mere 'being'" (Gatens 2003, 282).

Here, then, we have arrived at a radically different reading of de Beauvoir, as her model of becoming a woman now involves something that is *not* to be grasped with social constructivism (gender defines sex).[5] By not ascribing to biological essentialism (sex defines gender) either, de Beauvoir opens the way for a performative understanding of ontology, or better yet, of *ontogenesis*. de Beauvoir introduces a sexual differing, the fulcrum of which, we want to propose, is to be found in her concept "flesh." In *The Second Sex*, flesh is one of those singular points at which the conceptual and the creative meet. It is a term usually associated with Georges Bataille, Antonin Artaud, and Maurice Merleau-Ponty, who also make use of it in order to come closer to the morphogenetic essence of the human body. With de Beauvoir the concept functions as the point of departure from which she taps into the ongoing rewriting of sexual difference, since flesh allows her to traverse the signs that stick to the body, that decide the "situation of woman." In the end—and this is crucial—conceptualizing flesh allows her to be undecidable about the relations between the sexes that are to come.

First she provides a diagnosis of sexual difference via flesh, or incarnation, engaging herself with the psychoanalytical idea of the phallus.[6] The phallus involves signification—"the apprehension of a signification through an analogue of the signifying object" (de Beauvoir [1949] 2010, 56). Signification is the source of alienation: "the anxiety of his freedom leads the subject to search for himself in things, which is a way to flee from himself" (ibid., 57). This process of "bad faith" differs for the two sexes. For man, "the fleshy incarnation of transcendence" (ibid.) happens through the flesh of the penis, whereas woman "does not alienate herself in a graspable thing, does not reclaim herself: she is thus led to make her entire self an object, to posit herself as the Other" (ibid., 57–8). So whereas de Beauvoir immediately reminds us that "[o]nly within the situation grasped in its totality does anatomical privilege found a truly human privilege" (ibid., 58), the relation between the sexes is dualist when considering the phallus. In the context of the phallus or the totem, women can do nothing but "perpetuat[e] carnal existence" (ibid., 82) whereas men can incarnate transcendence via the phallus, a dualism which has asymmetrical consequences:

> Woman is sometimes designated as 'sex': it is she who is the flesh, its delights and its dangers. That for woman it is man who is sexed and carnal is a truth that has never been proclaimed

> because there is no one to proclaim it. The representation of
> the world as the world itself is the work of men; they describe
> it from a point of view that is their own and that they confound
> with the absolute truth. [...] since the coming of patriarchy, life
> in man's eyes has taken on a dual aspect: it is consciousness,
> will, transcendence, it is intellect; and it is matter, passivity,
> immanence, it is flesh (ibid., 162–3).

The current representation of sexual difference, de Beauvoir shows, is projected back into the past—as if sexual binarism precedes and thus justifies patriarchy, and as if young girls are destined to become woman.

Second, the way out of sexual difference (that is, the road to sexual differing) presents itself equally in *The Second Sex* through the flesh, and we have already seen this in our discussion of eroticism. Only by starting with the flesh, de Beauvoir moves towards an Irigarayan undecidability of sexual difference, a *true* becoming woman. Examples of this are the experiences of women in natural environments. In women's literature, among other things, de Beauvoir has found instances that, away from the house and the city, "show the comfort the adolescent girl finds in the fields and woods" (ibid., 376), which leads her to the important claim that here:

> [e]xistence is not only an abstract destiny inscribed in town
> hall registers; it is future and carnal richness. Having a body
> no longer seems like a shameful failing [...] Flesh is no longer
> filth: it is joy and beauty. Merged with sky and heath, the girl
> is this vague breath that stirs up and kindles the universe,
> and she is every sprig of heather; an individual rooted in the
> soil and infinite consciousness, she is both spirit and life; her
> presence is imperious and triumphant like that of the earth itself
> (ibid., 376–7).

Much like Artaud (1971) and his use of flesh, de Beauvoir proposes to think from a very *naïve* stance, which is not romanticizing a kind of youthfulness (think for instance how the same argument can be found when she talks about the post-menopausal woman), nor do we need to undo or forget how the processes of subjectification, of becoming a woman, are at work in our lives (a kind of Aristophanic return). What she instead asks us to do is to *rethink* sexual difference from a very pragmatic or empirical point of view. In fact, de Beauvoir introduces us to a naïve *ethics* that, as its point of departure, is not willing to accept received sociobiological or socio-cultural differences between the sexes. As with Artaud, it is an ethics that starts from the soil within which a force of life that gives form to flesh and spirit is at work. In contrast to the way de Beauvoir is usually read in feminist theory, she takes here an affirmative stance, trying to think of feminism not as a *critical* but as a *vitalist* project.

Deleuze and Guattari ([1980] 1987, 276–7) appear to be very much inspired by de Beauvoir's materialist feminism of the flesh as they equate her becoming-woman with "the girl." It is a thoroughly vitalist concept that performs the hysteric reality of *all* bodies-to-come:

> Doubtless, the girl becomes a woman in the molar or organic sense. But conversely, becoming-woman or the molecular woman is the girl herself. [...] She never ceases to roam upon a body without organs. [...] Thus girls do not belong to an age group, sex, order, or kingdom: they slip in everywhere, between orders, acts, ages, sexes; they produce *n* molecular sexes on the line of flight in relation to the dualism machines they cross right through. The only way to get outside the dualisms is to be-between, to pass between. [...] It is not the girl who becomes a woman; it is becoming-woman that produces the universal girl.[7]

By opposing the molar to the molecular and by favoring this molecular stance, Deleuze and Guattari do the same as de Beauvoir: they favor becoming over being, they study movement and affect instead of signs and codes. Contrary to Butler, who seems to be chasing a molar narrative, Deleuze and Guattari affirm de Beauvoir (and Artaud) in proposing a feminism that is an equally materialist and equally vitalist search for de Beauvoir's fleshy future.

For it is no coincidence that de Beauvoir does not say that the girl becomes the woman. There is not a projection backwards of the woman, of sexual binarism, onto the girl. The sexed body of the girl is not fully captured by the word "woman." de Beauvoir says here that there is becoming from the girl to the woman. It is a naiveté to come, an Irigarayan undecidability. It is a discovery of the flesh that is always already taking place. The virtual (the girl: sexual differing) has reality without being actual (because we are subjected to femininity: sexual difference). de Beauvoir's practical philosophy, which culminates in the flesh, asks us to commit ourselves to an ethics of rethinking feminism from its most elementary basis.

What Is Practical Philosophy?

In an interview Guattari tells us how he and Deleuze worked with this life force they found in the work of Artaud and de Beauvoir, amongst others, by always starting their analysis with "desire." This is true not least place when they come to speak of the woman:

> If Gilles Deleuze and I have adopted the position of practically not speaking of sexuality, and instead speaking of desire, it's because we consider that the problems of life and creation are never reducible to physiological functions, reproductive functions, to some particular dimension of the body. They always involve elements that are either beyond the individual in the social or political field, or else before the individual level (Guattari and Rolnik [1982] 2008, 411).

By starting with desire, Guattari and Deleuze radically ward off the critical perspective that turned out to be so central to feminist theory built on the dominant (molar) reception of de Beauvoir. It places fundamental question marks after its emphasis on power, which they replaced by an emphasis on desire. Power ascribes to the representationalism underlying sexual difference, whereas with desire the qualitative shift towards sexual differing can be made. Only in a short comment regarding the work of Michel Foucault, Deleuze (1997, 186) explains in a nutshell this important shift when claiming:

> In short, it is not the *dispositifs* of power that assemble [*agenceraient*], nor would they be constitutive; it is rather the *agencements* of desire that would spread throughout the formations of power following one of their dimensions.

Again, though we are now mainly concerned with feminist theory and sexual difference, this argument not only shifts the critical perspective as practiced in gender studies, it also offers an alternative to the way in which concepts like "race"/ethnicity, class, and age have been dominating the discussions within other fields in the humanities and the social sciences since the 1980's.

Let us first of all ensure that this concept of desire, which traverses the aforementioned categories and which might give one the impression that only the mind is now at stake (and not the body), is actually a materialist concept with Deleuze and Guattari. For although Guattari especially has a strong background in (Lacanian) psychoanalysis, their idea of desire is without a doubt Spinozist. Spinoza, and most of all the Spinoza of the *Ethics*, might very well be considered the first (the foremost) new materialist. Especially his formula—being the mind is an idea of the body, while the body is the object of the mind—is undisputedly the starting point of all new materialist thinking, and it has for that reason appeared in various guises throughout the work of new materialists. Spinoza's definition of desire starts from the sameness of the mind and body as it composes our nature, or as he puts it:

> All our efforts or desires follow from the necessity of our nature in such a manner that they can be understood either through it alone as their proximate cause, or in so far as we are a part of nature, which part cannot be adequately conceived through itself and without the other individuals (Spinoza [1677] 2001, E4App.1).

Desire, according to Spinoza and to Deleuze and Guattari, thus points at an *essence* that is formed in terms of the body and the mind created in its relation to other individuals which it is either affected by (that gives it joy) or that it tries to move away from (that offers it sadness). Of course, essence with Spinoza and Deleuze and Guattari is never the biological determinist type of essence re-affirmed in contemporary scholarship. It is a concept that allows them to express how our nature is taking up a form that necessarily re-creates itself in its relations to others, *ad infinitum*.

Essence equals the desiring flesh that does not know (yet) of sexual difference. Essence is a cut-out in nature (as de Beauvoir would put it), and equally within God (as Spinoza would put it) that acts as one, yet always in relation to how it pertains to others, and vice versa. The emphasis on desire and essence, then, does not deny the existence of male and female, of sexual difference, but instead denounces the ignorance with which epistemologies have folded into nature and cut it up into genus and species. A vitalist emphasis on desire, essence and the flesh, allows us to rethink such categorizations in a most revolutionary way. Indeed a Spinozist or Deleuzo-Guattarian perspective, as it claims that the essence is determined by what affects the thing and by how it is affected, starts from how life is being formed and how categories like sexual difference are created in it by the actions of the mind *and* the body.

Such an affirmative vitalism allows us to rethink feminism (and all other minor fields in cultural theory) not by critiquing the "being" of a woman, but rather by affirming the molecular ways in which the body and mind can be conceptualized as "female" in how they are created (as one), or in how they affect and are affected. That is why Deleuze and Guattari ([1980] 1987, 291), re-reading de Beauvoir, claim that a becoming-woman "necessarily affects men just as much as women." That is why the girl deterritorializes all forms of life (as well as the non-organic). For just as a becoming Jewish affects the non-Jew as it affects the Jew, as they stated before this last quote, men also, in the ongoing questioning of their essence, enter the trajectories of "femininity" as it moves them away from the dominant (molar) socio-cultural (male-oriented) stance from which society is organized. Starting with the body, with the affections that befall the body and how they present us with ideas in the mind (see e.g. Spinoza [1677] 2001, E2P16), this then allows us a radical complexification of the asymmetry indicated by de Beauvoir, "For the two sexes imply a multiplicity of molecular combinations bringing into play not only the man in the woman and the woman in the man, but the relation of each to the animal, the plant, etc.: a thousand tiny sexes" (Deleuze and Guattari [1980] 1987, 213).

Deleuze ([1981] 1988, 124) already noted that "[...] if you define bodies and thoughts as capacities for affecting and being affected, many things change." In terms of its consequences for feminism, Grosz (1994) sees this as the starting point for a way of rethinking sexual difference not as a meaning imposed upon bodies, but as the expression of bodies (earlier we called this material-discursive). In other words, sexual differing is about the way the body is able to sediment itself or form itself within the socio-cultural according to the practices in which it acts:

> So an animal, a thing is never separable from its relations with the world. The interior is only a selected exterior, and the exterior, a projected interior. The speed and slowness of metabolisms, perceptions, actions and reactions, link together to constitute a particular individual in the world (Deleuze [1981] 1988, 125).

In sum, then, the move from sexual difference, as it has dominated feminism over the past half-century, to sexual differing, as we can already find in de Beauvoir, means an emphasis on the *agencements* of desire and the way they allow us to think of the flesh and its nature in the way it becomes actualized and realized within practices. Then power is an action upon an action, as Foucault already put it. Or rather, power sets itself to the structuring of the socio-cultural by means of prohibition, as Claire Colebrook describes it. For she claims: "There is only a phallus rather than a penis, through the process of collective inscription" (Colebrook 2002, 134). This materialist stance does not want to critique collective (molar) inscription, but rather asks us how, in life, the creation of the woman (and the man) comes about in the (mute, fleshy, molecular) affects to which these collective inscriptions *respond*.

From Sexual Difference to Sexual Differing

Let us end with a close reading of the conclusion to *The Second Sex*, as it is here that de Beauvoir's practical philosophy comes to full fruition. In the text, de Beauvoir ([1949] 2010, 758) is truly opening up for a sexual differing, a pushing of sexual difference to the extreme, because she claims that neither men nor women have so far been willing to "assum[e] all the consequences of this situation that one proposes and the other undergoes." What happens when we do assume all the consequences of sexual difference? When we no longer critique the collective inscription of sexual difference, but ask an affirmative question instead?

First, de Beauvoir states that "today's woman is torn between the past and the present" (ibid., 761). She is torn, that is, between collective inscriptions, and the linear, causal theory of time with which they work, and creative evolution, which, speaking with Henri Bergson, comes with the vitual/actual, with *durée* as it opens up a world to come. The collective inscriptions need not be critiqued as in equality or postmodern feminism, but one must ask to what materialist, fleshy desires these collective inscriptions respond. Patriarchy utilizes what it finds for its own self-perpetuation. But a revolutionary feminism does not have a model. We could say that for women, the molding into utilities of affects, of life forces leads to a being torn between past and present, between sexual difference and sexual differing. And this is actually something we can affirm, as it shows how sexual difference implies sexual differing all along. de Beauvoir describes the situation as follows:

> [M]ost often, she appears as a 'real woman' disguised as a man, and she feels as awkward in her woman's body as in her masculine garb. She has to shed her old skin and cut her own clothes. She will only be able to do this if there is a collective change. No one teacher can today shape a 'female human being' that would be an exact homologue to the 'male human being': if raised like boy, the young girl feels she is an exception, and that subjects her to a new kind of specification (ibid.).

An upbringing like a boy and masculine clothing (that is to say, emancipation) is what de Beauvoir's woman wants to move away from, similar to the way in which she wants to move away from an unemancipated world. Neither the inscriptions of equality feminism nor those of an androcentric world fit her flesh. Woman, according to de Beauvoir, has to rid herself of these inscriptions. This means, following an ethics of affirmation, that *she has to cut her own clothes*. Despite the dominant reception of her work even in French feminism, de Beauvoir thus clearly speaks the language of difference. As she states:

> Woman is defined neither by her hormones nor by mysterious instincts but by the way she grasps, through foreign consciousness, her body and her relation to the world [...] it would be impossible to keep woman from being what she *was made*, and she will always trail this past behind her; if the weight of this past is accurately measured, it is obvious that her destiny is not fixed in eternity (ibid., 761; original emphasis).

This fragment, even though it has been read as existentialism *par excellence*, is not only crystal clear about collective inscriptions. It also clarifies how we could read the evolution de Beauvoir alluded to in the previously given quote. This evolution—which after postmodern feminism seems wholly individualized in this fragment, but throughout *The Second Sex* appears as (equally) collective—we can read in a manner similar to how we read de Beauvoir's interpretation of young girls' naiveté. Equality feminism is a narrative of progress, predicated on the coupling possible/real, on a linear and causal theory of time. It wants sexual difference to be solved once and for all. Difference feminism thinks of emancipation differently: "To emancipate woman is to refuse to enclose her in the relations she sustains with man, but not to deny them" (ibid., 766). The latter feminism allows for bringing along the past that shadows woman for life; it has gotten rid of the habit of narratives of progress, and speaks the language of true duration, of becoming a thousand tiny sexes, of sexual differing.

Where, then, is this new conceptualization of emancipation to be found? It is not to be found in our fearful imaginings of a future *without* sexual difference, because, says de Beauvoir: "Let us beware lest our lack of imagination impoverish the future; the future is only an abstraction for us; each one of us secretly laments the absence in it of what was" (ibid., 765). de Beauvoir does not want women to be confined by sexual difference, nor does she want to deny them relations with men. Although it has often been remarked in feminist scholarship that de Beauvoir seems to say that *men* are to liberate women by giving up their privileges, our reading of de Beauvoir suggests an alternative take on the following, oft-discredited fragment, in which she ends her masterpiece by saying:

> *Within the given world*, it is up to man to make the reign of freedom triumph; to carry off this supreme victory, men and women must, among other things and *beyond their natural differentiations*, unequivocally affirm their brotherhood (ibid., 766; emphasis added).

What we see here is that it is *in* sexual difference that we can find *sexual differing*. Sexual difference is nothing but a collective molar habit of mind, and, up until the conclusion, *The Second Sex* has described this habit as well as where it undid itself. Sexual differing is not found in the future, but between the linguistic codes of sexual difference where it always already roams, materially and vitally.

Notes

1. For the intrinsic link between these exemplifications, see van der Tuin (2009).
2. Note, however, that Heinämaa (1997, 27) reads this phenomenology as breaking through the nature/culture divide. She also states that with de Beauvoir as well as Butler we can break through the divide between the mental and the bodily (ibid., 22).
3. Let us state clearly that we are aware of the fierce criticism that the received view of de Beauvoir in general, and of *The Second Sex* in particular, has received from feminist scholars in both the United States and Europe. We are also aware of the translation problem surrounding *The Second Sex* prior to when Constance Borde and Sheila Malovany-Chevallier's 2010 translation appeared. A huge body of work has been produced around these issues that is impossible to reference even when one privileges, with Donna Haraway, a partial perspective. We thus refrain from the referencing, albeit that these discussions form the background of this chapter. It might be argued that this chapter is to be placed in the tradition of post-poststructuralist scholarship on de Beauvoir, as Sonia Kruks (2005, 290) calls it, moving beyond biological essentialism and social constructivism indeed. It might also be seen as an attempt to move out of another double bind that is so often to be found around de Beauvoir. Attempts to free *The Second Sex* from Sartre often confine the text to another Master, and, consequently, it is again not subjected to a close reading (ibid., 294).
4. Feminist scholarship dismissing or criticizing the paradoxes in the work of de Beauvoir is rampant. Although many scholars try to affirm the paradoxes as a necessary part of de Beauvoir's feminist philosophy, it is hardly ever affirmed that these paradoxes actually are (her) feminism. For very recent examples, see Changfoot (2009a, 2009b).
5. Note that by not accepting the sex/gender distinction as a key to *The Second Sex*, we arrive at conclusions that differ from those of Hughes and Witz (1997).
6. Remember that de Beauvoir is as ambiguous about Marxism as she is about psychoanalysis. Throughout *The Second Sex*, both are subscribed to for their accurate

descriptions as well as utopianism and critiqued for their genderblindness. The virtue of the latter, in particular, is that it proposes that "the existent is a body" (de Beauvoir [1949] 2010, 68), even that

> [t]he existent is a sexed body; in its relations with other existents that are also sexed bodies, sexuality is thus always involved (ibid., 55).

7. Bergson ([1907] 1998, 313) makes the same argument concerning a boy which supports Deleuze's argument all the more. His version runs as follows:

> The truth is that if language here were molded on reality, we should not say 'The child becomes the man,' but 'There is becoming from the child to the man.' [...] In the second proposition, 'becoming' is a subject. It comes to the front. It is the reality itself; childhood and manhood are then only possible stops, mere views of the mind; we now have to do with the objective movement itself [...].

Chapter 8
The End of (Wo)Man

Although so far we have discussed large portions of the humanities, we have focused in particular on feminist theory. We have demonstrated how new materialism is being developed here, and how feminist theory allows us to rewrite the most common intellectual history in order to create concepts and produce insights that are less distortedly based on (gendered) hierarchies. Subsequently, these insights are less dependent on gaps between culture and nature, language and materiality, and body and mind—not by doing away with them, but by pushing them to the extreme. Due to the fact that "substance dualism" has been diagnosed as one of the most prominent ca(u)ses of gendering since Simone de Beauvoir's seminal *The Second Sex* ([1949] 2010), feminist theory is one of the key sites of critical reflection upon substance dualism. Such reflection, if we can call it that, is also a key to the development of the new materialism. Yet feminist theory is not about critique, and therewith about reflection. As in many other parts of academia, one of the defining *creative* features of feminism in academia is its focus on theories of the subject (Braidotti 1991, 164). Albeit that this focus can easily be historically substantiated with a reference to women's explicit exclusion from academic knowledge production until the late nineteenth century in most Western countries, the implied *anthropocentrism* does not suit new materialism's metaphysics. It is even questionable whether substance dualism can be overcome epistemologically, because the defining feature of epistemology seems to be the presupposed hierarchical split between the subject and the object, and therewith the split between epistemology (knowing) and ontology (being). How then can the main conceptual creation in feminist theory be defined so that a new materialism gets to be fully enfleshed? In this chapter we will propose that not all (feminist) theories of the subject imply a human-subject-centered epistemology, as our interviewees in Part One have already shown us. Mapping a new materialism by re-writing *these* theories is key to this final chapter.

Sandra Harding's *The Science Question in Feminism* from 1986, which is the standard reference text in feminist epistemology, does perform an anthropocentrism. Notwithstanding the fact that Donna Haraway's famous response to Harding in "Situated Knowledges: *The Science Question in Feminism* and the Privilege of Partial Perspective" discussed its limits and offered us a new feminist materialism as early as 1988, via concepts such as the "material-semiotic actor" and the "apparatus of bodily production" (Haraway 1988, 595), feminist epistemology in general has always been structured by the desire to make clear that humanism is in fact an androcentrism in need of alternatives. "Feminist standpoint theory" and "feminist postmodernism" are both examples of this move. In the former case a specific "woman's way of knowing" was proposed, while in the latter, following a pluralization act, a plethora of women's ways of knowing was put to the fore in order to shift gross generalizations about the nature and culture of women (Harding 1986, 1991). The fact that even feminist postmodernism has not been able to shift such humanism owing to a dualist response to both androcentrism and feminist standpoint theory, and has confined itself to an anthropocentric linguisticism as a result, has been demonstrated by Claire Colebrook's "Postmodernism is a Humanism: Deleuze and Equivocity" from 2004, which was discussed in earlier chapters. The fundamental claim in that article is that

> [o]ne must recognize oneself as this or that gendered identity in order to take part in what [Judith] Butler refers to as the heterosexual matrix; but, precisely because this matrix is constituted through speech, acts and performatives, it is also always capable of being rendered otherwise, of producing new relations (Colebrook 2004, 292–3)

This outlines the fact that linguisticism (language, and "the interstices of language" as they reveal themselves with language, to use Butler's concepts) as well as anthropocentrism are equally reductive results owing to a dualist argumentation (cf. Kirby 1997, 2006, 2011). We have spent enough time in earlier chapters of this part of the book situating and re-writing any linguisticism and the way its practitioners consider materiality intrinsically semiotic (that is, in itself mute) the time has now come for a radical elimination of any anthropocentrism from our materialism.

Here we might hook up with an early and apt diagnosis of the anthropocentrism that manifests itself in the aforementioned dualist response to a supposedly inclusive but in fact profoundly androcentric humanism that can be found in Genevieve Lloyd's "Preface to the Second Edition" of the seminal *The Man of Reason* (originally published in 1984). Following the methodological gesture of contrasting Cartesian dualism and Spinozist monism, Lloyd ([1984] 1993, xii-xiii; original emphasis) claims as follows:

> What must be the relation between minds and bodies for it to be possible for the symbolic content of *man* and *woman* to feed into the formation of our sense of ourselves as male or female? [...] Spinoza's *rapprochement* between reason and passion can [...] be seen as a point where the grip of male-female symbolism might have been broken. And his treatment of the mind as an idea of the body suggests a starting point, too, for a clearer understanding of how the meanings given to bodies can be both metaphorical and rightly experienced as 'real' differences.

Contrary to feminist (post)modernism, Lloyd thus asks how a gendered (dualist) organization and a linguisticism *emerge from* a monist multiplicity, just like Alphonso Lingis (1994), Arun Saldanha (2006), and Michael Hames-García (2008) ask how a racial linguisticism emerges from the same flux. Although in the present book we do not equate new materialism's metaphysics with a Spinozism, *monism* has run like an electrical current through our conceptualization. It is monist metaphysics that truly shifts anthropocentrism, and which is at work in one way or another in the materialisms of the authors discussed in this final chapter.[1]

Recently, cultural theory's monist take on culture and nature, language and materiality, and body and mind has stirred an abundance of neologisms. These neologisms provide a first insight into the monist proposal, always in keeping with Lyotard's, Deleuze's, and Latour's rewriting of modernity (see Chapter 6 above), to provide a non-anthropocentric mapping of the morphogenetic changes of the real. Let us give two examples. Karen Barad in *Meeting the Universe Halfway: Quantum Physics and the Entanglement of Matter and Meaning* from 2007 has coined the term "intra-action." Barad (2007, 33; cf. Barad 2010, 244) writes that "in contrast to the usual "interaction," which assumes that there are separate individual agencies that precede their interaction, the notion of intra-action recognizes that distinct agencies [...] emerge through, their intra-action." This process ontology shifts an atomist metaphysics of pre-existing entities, and suggests a world which Haraway (2003: 6), alluding to the work of Alfred North Whitehead, has been characterized as one in which "[b]eings do not preexist their relatings." Similar to Lloyd's, Lingis', Saldanha's and Hames-García's question after the emergence of a gendered/racialized (dualist) organization from a monist multiplicity, Barad (2010, 254) states explicitly "intra-actions necessarily entail constitutive exclusions, which constitute an irreducible openness," which is not only to say that dualism can only happen within monism, and not the other way around, but also that dualism is never fully fixed. This is why Barad, while reading Niels Bohr through Jacques Derrida, terms ontology a "hauntology." Barad frees Derrida from a possible linguisticist interpretation, just as Vicki Kirby (2011) does, since hauntology prefers neither the mind (or the immaterial, cultural, linguistic) nor the body (or the muted material, the natural). It is therefore non-anthropocentric, insofar it works with an ontology of "the world's radical aliveness" (Barad 2007, 33). Starting from the spectral and shadows that are "constitutive without belonging to" (Kochhar-Lindgren 2011, 25) the material, does not affirm the dualist desire to try to represent and thus the possibility of fully capturing the world while being radically separate from it. On the contrary, hauntology necessarily *includes* all of the unforeseen (un-human) radical powers.

A second example can be found in the work of Manuel DeLanda, whose "morphogenesis" from "The Geology of Morals: A Neo-Materialist

Interpretation" (1996) we borrowed in this book. In *A Thousand Years of Nonlinear History* DeLanda (1997, 32; original emphasis) speaks of "meshworks" in order to maintain a differentiation between "self-organized *meshworks* of diverse elements" and "*hierarchies* of uniform elements" which "not only coexist and intermingle, [but...] give rise to one another." The creation of the concept of the meshwork, which equals the "collective" composed of "hybrids" coined in *We Have Never Been Modern* of Bruno Latour ([1991] 1993, 47), is part of a monist metaphysics. In *A New Philosophy of Society* DeLanda (2006, 6) says to focus on "the movement that in reality generates all these emergent wholes" in which "language plays an important but not a constitutive role" (ibid., 3). Furthermore, DeLanda makes clear that "the properties of a whole cannot be reduced to those of its parts [because] they are the result not of an aggregation of the components' own properties but of the actual exercise of their capabilities" (ibid., 11). DeLanda (2002, 4) thus introduces a concept that not only "grants reality full autonomy from the human mind" but also one that comes very close to the neologisms put to work by Barad. DeLanda's work demonstrates how Barad's suggested *contrast* between inter- and intra-action is a methodological step. The dualism seemingly suggested is introduced in order to retain intra-action.

Apart from it being a rewriting, the introduction of neologisms does not aim at exchanging a seemingly "wrong" academic terminology for a terminology with which the world can be captured "better." Such an epistemic stance would presuppose a subject independent of an object, and such a representationalist hierarchy or gap does not fit the proposed monist metaphysics. Combining Whitehead's "event" and Deleuze's "sense," Mike Halewood (2009, 50) in "Language, Subjectivity and Individuality" states: "the world creates (or constructs) sense as an effect of the interrelation of singularities within the virtual. Given that all subjects are part of this world they are also created within such creativity." Here we clearly see that the subject according to a monist metaphysics is a consequence rather than the full-fledged starting point of an epistemic experience. Albeit that Barad (2010, 247, 253) with "queer causality" warns us against any easy opposition to linear causality due to haunting, this departure from the prioritization of the subject breaks through anthropocentrism, and proposes a non-anthropocentric take on what supposedly forms the core of what is human (language, and subjectivity). Deleuze's "The tree greens" (1990, 21 in Halewood 2009, 51) and Whitehead's "We enjoy the green foliage of the spring greenly" (1967, 251 in ibid.) propose that greenness itself is an active expression, and that we *prehend* the greenness of the tree. It is the state of affairs that enables language, and this language or expression is not just human. Whitehead in *Process and Reality* ([1929/1978] 1985, 52) states that he has "adopted the term 'prehension,' to express the activity whereby an actual entity effects its own concretion of other things" which shows once more that the metaphysics proposed here is not an anthropocentric linguisticism. First, the focus is on the activity, process, event, and, second, cause and effect have been "queered" vis-à-vis a dualist metaphysics.

Let us now fully immerse ourselves in the non-anthropocentric metaphysics of new materialism. Therefore we will read Michel Foucault's birth and death of the subject via a discussion of parts of his secondary thesis, recently published as *Introduction to Kant's Anthropology* from 2008 (though the thesis was submitted in 1961). Foucault addresses the question of how anthropocentrism has shaped dualism, and how it has in fact distorted our (representationalist) strategies of studying the real. Quentin Meillassoux, who, in *After Finitude* ([2006] 2008) re-reads Kant as well, offers us a different (yet equally non-humanist, non-anthropocentric) way out compared with Foucault's famous thesis, as we have already seen in our interview with him in the first part of this book (Chapter 4). Putting the (dis-) connection between Foucault and Meillassoux at center stage in order to show in what directions new materialism's anti-anthropocentrism leads us, we will then open up the notion of subjectivity by reading a mathematics in materialist thinking. Speculative materialism or realism, as it is being developed by Meillassoux, but also by Ray Brassier and Graham Harman (Bryant et al, eds. 2011), is then diffractively read with those new materialist scholars who are big in science studies today, several of whom have already been discussed in previous chapters of this book: DeLanda, Barad, Kirby, and Brian Massumi. By involving mathematics (set theory, geometry, topology) as a means of breaking open the Kantian definitions of epistemology and ontology, we are offered important new materialist claims that (implicitly) push those fundamental humanist oppositions—like (wo) man—to the extreme. After all, science studies has been characterized as being an *anthropology* on/with objects (Mol 2002, 32), and thus has been implicitly criticized for an ongoing focus on the Kantian (subjectivist) problematic while trying to dualistically move away from epistemology as a representationalist practice (ibid., vii).

The Birth of the Subject = The Death of the Subject

(Part of) Foucault's project has been to understand the coming into being of the sciences of man (Foucault [1966/1970] 1994). Immanuel Kant, that is, the anthropological turn in philosophy that started with Kant, is being rewritten in Foucault's work. For Foucault, the birth of the subject *equals* the death of the subject, or in a Nietzschean mode, the death of God equals the death of *man*. Foucault states in his *Introduction* that an unfinished and unpublished correspondence with Kant's (former) student Jakob Sigismund Beck in conjunction with the published version of the former's *Anthropology from a Pragmatic Point of View* from 1798 makes clear that Kant managed

> [...] to define the space which an anthropology, in general, could occupy: a space in which self-observation bears not upon the subject as such, nor upon the pure 'I' of the synthesis, but upon "a 'I'" that is object and present *solely* in its *singular* phonenemal [sic] truth. But this "'I'-object," [...] is no stranger to the determining subject; for it is ultimately nothing more than the subject as it is affected by itself. [The space of anthropology] is entirely taken over by the presence of a deaf, unbound, and often errant freedom which operates in the domain of originary passivity (Foucault 2008, 39; original emphasis).

Foucault notes that the Preface to the *Anthropology* states that Kant's object was "what man makes of himself—or can and should make of himself—as a free-acting being" (Foucault 2008, 44) thus making anthropology pragmatic. Anthropology deals with the balancing act in which "man is considered to be a "citizen of the world," as belonging, that is, to the realm of the concrete universal, in which the legal subject is determined by and submits to certain laws, but is at the same time a human being who, in his or her freedom, acts according to a universal moral code" (ibid., 42). And it shows "how a juridical relationship of the order of a possession, which is to say a *jus rerum*, manages to preserve the moral kernel of a person construed as a free subject" (ibid.). Pragmatics then deals not with human nature or essence, but with "a movement where nature and freedom are bound up in the *Gebrauch*—one of the meanings of which is given in the word 'usage'" (ibid., 51). To be more precise, "in *Anthropology*, man is neither a *homo natura*, nor a purely free subject; he is caught by the syntheses already operated by his relationship to the world" (ibid., 54–5). Studying a different set of concepts (*Gemüt* and *Geist*) allows Foucault to claim that in the *Anthropology* no space is given, however, to "being tied to the passivity of phenomenal determinations" (ibid., 63) since

> The *Geist* is [...] the principle, in the *Gemüt*, of a de-dialecticized, nontranscendental dialectic oriented towards the domain of experience and playing an integral part in the play of phenomena itself. It is the *Geist* which offers the *Gemüt* the freedom of the possible, stripping it of its determinations, and providing it with a future which it owes to nothing but itself (ibid.).

On this basis, Foucault comes to claim that the "I"/Subject of the *Kritik* is wholly inverted in the *Anthropology*, in a way that is more complex than an exchange of cause and effect. Namely "it appears in the density of a becoming where its sudden emergence infallibly assumes the retrospectively constituted meaning of the already there" (ibid., 67).

In the introduction to the *Logik*, published in 1800 (nearly twenty years after his first *Kritik*) Kant famously summarizes his critical project in not three, but four questions. He summarized his three critiques by asking himself "what can I know?," "what should I do?," and "what may I hope for?." He then added a fourth question to the list, namely: "what is man?" Only in his later notes (*Notes and Fragments* (2005)) he realizes that this sentence in fact captured his main contribution to thought. For whereas in those days it was still common to start thinking first and foremost from a thorough conceptualization of God, from which thoughts on nature and on the human being subsequently arose, Kant started his philosophy with the human being—or even better, with human thought and its relation to nature. In other words, Kant turned (theological) metaphysics into transcendental anthropology. Kant's second Copernican revolution, as it revolves around concepts like the Subject, *Geist* and *Gemüt*, was by all means a humanist revolution, since it turned the relations between the three poles mentioned around. This is clearly noted by Foucault (2008, 78):

> At last man emerges as universal synthesis, forming a real unity in which the personality of God and the objectivity of the world are rejoined, the sensible principle and the *supra* sensible; and man becomes the mediatory from which "*einer absoluter Ganze*" takes shape. It is from the starting point of man that the absolute can be thought.

Foucault claims that it is with Kant that man has not only turned into the origin of thought, but that both God and the world (nature) subsequently arise. Yet as "[...] man immediately defines himself as a citizen of the world, as '*Weltbewohner*': '*Der Mensch gehört zwar mit zur Welt.*' And completing the circle, all reflection on man involves reflection on the world" (ibid., 78–9), Foucault makes clear that this does not involve a naturalism ("where a science of man implies a knowledge of nature," ibid. 79) nor a determinism "on the level of the phenomena" (ibid.) but rather "it is the development of self-awareness and of the 'I am': the subject self-affecting by the movement in which he becomes aware of himself as an object" (ibid.). This affirmative rewriting of Kant, contrary to how Meillassoux reads Kant (as we will see later) boils down to what we could call, with Barad, an intra-action between (social) world and Subject. Foucault even states that "the world, as a whole (*Ganz*)" seems to be excluded from language, yet has structure or meaning (ibid., 80). The way in which he then explains the world comes close to DeLanda's immanent morphogenetic changes of the real, where the world is source, domain, and limit (ibid., 80–1). That is to say, the metaphysics according to which Foucault re-writes Kant is wholly monist: "the whole of existence defines what belongs to it necessarily and originarily" (ibid., 84). The death of the Subject is encapsulated in its Kantian birth.

Anthropocentrism (Un)Solved, or: Critiquing Critique

In *After Finitude*, Meillassoux takes on a similar project as Foucault, which we might summarize as a rewriting of Kantian paradigms that concern the human being (the Subject) and the object. Yet he does so by asking a different opening question. Foucault is interested in Kant from what we might call a post-Nietzschean perspective. For although a historian, Foucault's call for the End of Man is about a resistance against the Absolute powers from the pre-critical period, as they keep haunting man and the way in which man conceptualizes his newfound rationality. Foucault sets himself to a discovering of *empirical reason*, what Foucault earlier referred to as a pragmatics, and it is thus that he wants to push Kant's dualist thinking to the limit. Foucault already notices this emphasis on the empirical in Kant himself when Foucault (2008, 63) summarizes Kant's final steps: "The movement which, in the *Critique*, gave rise to the transcendental mirage is extended and prolonged in the *Anthropology* in the form of the empirical, concrete life of the *Gemüt*."

In the preface to *After Finitude*, Alain Badiou claims that Meillassoux's approach to the three questions that summarize Kant's *Critiques*, rather than re-reading their dynamics in the empirical, pushes them to the point of a "critique of Critique" (Badiou in Meillassoux [2006] 2008, vii) which is to say that Kantian anthropocentrism has not at all been "solved" by Foucault or his followers. For whereas the first and foremost Kantian question ("what can I know?") has been attacked primarily (by Foucault for instance) for its use of the "I am," or, the construction of Subjectivity (the "I think") which it entails, Meillassoux's critique of Critique focuses on the necessity of "knowledge" and the way Kant's notion of knowledge is built on an odd kind of dualism. Foucault (2008, 78) already noticed clearly that "it is from the starting point of man that the absolute can be thought" and it is this idea in particular that Meillassoux considers corrupt. Thus, without doing away with the subject and the object (he actually affirms it rigorously), the latter sets himself to a rethinking of how this opposition relates to one another in terms of knowledge.

In Kant, Meillassoux sees a metaphysics being developed which he refers to as "correlationism." He defines it as such: "Correlationism consists in disqualifying the claim that it is possible to consider the realms of subjectivity and objectivity independently of one another" (Meillassoux [2006] 2008, 5). Meillassoux does not negate correlationism as such; later in his work it is in fact *through* "weak correlationism" that he sets up the necessity of his speculative materialism. But the way in which Kant introduced correlationism in his *Kritik der reinen Vernunft* in 1781 was, as Meillassoux ([2006] 2008, 124) calls it, a "catastrophe" for philosophy.

Crucial for Kant's correlationism is the idea that the objects in the world consist in themselves, *independent* of any observation, and at the same time have subjective qualities that allow them to reveal themselves *in an observation* (ibid., 31). For a human being, then, the things in themselves are not knowable but we can think them; whereas we can get rational knowledge (about a thing) only in the observation, in how the object allows itself to be represented. It is thus that the world as a whole (*das Ganze*) subjectively comes into being, from the perspective of the "I am." Meillassoux's critique of this Kantian relation between subject and object is twofold. First, he questions the *limits* that Kant puts to rational knowledge. Why can't the object itself be known? How can thought ever be given "limited access" to the object (which thus in the presentation allows itself to be thought but not to be known)? Secondly, he asks himself why Kant demands the object to be presented in order for it to be thought. This notion of givenness (the object has to be confronted with the subject in order to become part of the world) also sounds questionable because it is deeply anthropocentric.

In order to clarify his reservations, Meillassoux gives us the example of what he calls the "arche-fossil" (a life that has ceased to be before the human being and its thinking came into existence) or the question of the ancestral. He wonders whether it could be possible, as Kantian thinking seems to presuppose, that "Science can think a world wherein spatio-temporal givenness itself came into being within a time and a space which preceded every variety of givenness" (ibid., 22). Or, how is correlationism liable to interpret ancestral statements? The answer of course is that it (philosophically) cannot, which is a serious critique of Kant and of the anthropocentrism that he proposes. The paleobiologist confronted with the arche-fossil has a problem thinking ancestral space-time that never "appeared" to him and to which he thus has no access (since it does not take place). Meillassoux's critique of Critical (correlationist) thinking is a critique not of the *being* but of the *knowing* Subject. His alternative is a speculative metaphysics, which is not subjective, but rather demands that philosophy turn to objectivity again. The critique of Critique is thus a critique of epistemology as we know it.

Doing this he also comes back to God and the tripartite taxonomy of thought discussed earlier. Contrary to Foucault, whom we have called a post-Nietzschean, Meillassoux is by all means an *anti*-Nietzschean. For whereas Nietzsche, at the close of the nineteenth century claimed that the Age of Reason (introduced to us by Kant among others) has caused us to murder God, Meillassoux claims exactly the opposite. He states that Kantian thinking, in which the absolute has been closed off from thought for good, expelled from the metaphysical, has caused the remarkable *return* of religious fundamentalism today as it allowed for the absolute to be removed from knowing and thus to be revived in the form of believing (ibid., 45).

Both Foucault's and Nietzsche's comments are of course not correlationist, in Meillassoux's opinion. Rethinking the Kantian "I am" empirically, they push the whole subject-object opposition to the extreme, introducing us to a new kind of thinking that has been able to firmly rewrite correlationism. Meillassoux calls this thinking a "subjective metaphysics," which is all about absolutizing *the correlate itself*:

> A metaphysics of this type may select from among various forms of subjectivity, but it is invariably characterized by the fact that it hypostatizes some mental, sentient, or vital term: representation in the Leibnizian monad; Schelling's Nature, or the objective subject-object; Hegelian Mind; Schopenhauer's Will; the Will (or *Wills*) to Power in Nietzsche; perception loaded with memory in Bergson; Deleuze's Life, etc. (ibid., 37).

Meillassoux goes on defining this subjective metaphysics, in a mode that resembles the oppositional logic that we have discussed in chapter 6 of this book, and which also characterizes Barad's reading of hauntology as affirmed through Bohr's complementarity (Barad 2010, 253):

> Even in those cases where the vitalist hypostatization of the correlation (as in Nietzsche of Deleuze) is explicitly identified with a critique of 'the subject' or of 'metaphysics,' it shares

with speculative idealism the same twofold decision which ensures its irreducibility to naïve realism or some variant of transcendental idealism:

The concepts created by subjective metaphysics, as they are nowadays increasingly popular within cultural theory, create a metaphysics that we could also call a metaphysics of the event (referring to Whitehead). It has no eye for individual objects, or at least these individual objects do not exist in their entirety but only insofar as they are actualized in the event. And it is this actualization which in the end, as Leibniz put it, is the only possible world. Foucault can be accused in a sense of forgetting the object, but we will get back to this later.

It is important to understand that this twofold definition of subjective metaphysics makes any materialism *im*possible, as Meillassoux claims. Just before he confronts us with this definition of subjective metaphysics, which (as stated) cannot think the Epicurean atom, he says that Epicureanism is in fact the paradigm of all materialisms. In Epicureanism

> [...] thought can access the absolute nature of all things through the notions of atoms and void, and which asserts that *this nature is not necessarily correlated with an act of thought,* since thought exists only in an aleatory manner, being immanent to contingent atomic compounds (for the gods themselves are decomposable), which are in-essential for the existence of elementary natures (ibid., 36; emphasis added).

The speculative materialism that Meillassoux proposes seems very different from the materialisms discussed so far, as indeed it does *not* seem to underpin the Spinozist monism which we have been developing up till now.

When stating that absolute reality consists of entities without thought, or even of entities that necessarily precede thought (we now see why he started his argument with the arche-fossil, which indeed turns into the perfect example of an event preceding human thought), he radically does away with Spinoza's pantheism. According to Meillassoux, Spinoza's claim that God equals nature (since both are unlimited, they must be one) is a subjective metaphysical definition of God as it creates a larger whole which equals the absolute. Considering God as equivalent to nature also means that nature is rational (which, of course, paleobiologists also believe when they consider their readings of nature "real," as in, the same as the objective materiality) and this too is an impossible anthropocentrism to Meillassoux. For him nature is contingent, especially because it precedes thought, or even better, because it precedes *any system of logic* that we could come up with (see his argument on "spatio-temporal givenness," ibid., 22). Again in contrast with Spinozism, Meillassoux claims there is no such thing as the Principle of Sufficient Reason; every cause can have an endless amount of consequences and these consequences are in no way "given" in thought. In the end he therefore feels much closer to David Hume than to Kant's correlationism in which knowledge of any synthethic proposition can never be *a priori*. This manifest stability of chaos, Meillassoux argues, "[...] would allow us to penetrate much deeper into the nature of a temporality delivered from real necessity" (ibid., 101).

Pushing Kant's weak correlationism to the extreme, Meillassoux composes a speculative materialism that is quite different from Foucauldian and post-Nietzschean thought, but which is nevertheless of the greatest importance for the new materialist project. For although his fiercely argumentative rewriting of the history of philosophy comes up with quite a different cartography compared to the sketches we have produced in the previous chapters—his appreciation of Descartes is especially hard to combine with what has been said above—his moves away from anthropocentrism contribute a great deal to the project announced by Foucault.

Let us therefore take a closer look at the closing of his first chapter (and the start of the second) in which he discusses ancestrality. Here Meillassoux introduces us to the two grand speculative materialist themes. First, there is a radical break between objects (matter) and the thoughts that follow. With this claim, however, he does not accept linear space-time (which the word "follow" might suggest); he does away with linear space-time by stating: "to inscribe these conditions in time is to turn them into objects and hence to anthropologize them" (ibid., 23). The claim thus emphasizes the contingency of matter (nature, the object) and is interested in how thought is capable of accessing the uncorrelated, the world not-given.

Second, though it is not elaborated upon in *After Finitude* but employed as a recurring referent to speculative materialist futures, Meillassoux keeps stressing "mathematics' ability to discourse about the great outdoors; to discourse about a past where both humanity and life are absent" (ibid., 26).

The two "propositions" refer us once more to Spinoza and actually reveal a more similar approach. For although the first part of the *Ethics* elaborates on the existence of only One substance (which is necessarily both the absolute infinite God and Nature), it is immediately added that it holds in it the attributes (for instance a human being), and is organized in different modes (for instance thought and extension). Concerning the human being, mind and body are "the same thing" since they are the essence of the individual (and make up one attribute of God). This is sometimes referred to as Spinoza's parallelism (although the term comes from Leibniz), yet this term is probably a bit too "equivocal," as it seems to suggest a sort of similarity that cannot be observed. An important argument for its univocity is that although Spinoza claims that all that is action in the body is also action in the mind, an idea (an action of the mind) is a consequence of its body. This does not mean that the body can determine the mind to think (as the mind also cannot determine the body to move) ([1677] 2001, E3P2), it does mean that the body (*res extensa*) is what Brian Massumi (2002, 8) would call *ontologically prior* to the mind, since bodies "[...] have ontological privilege in the sense that they constitute the field of the emergence." Much as with Meillassoux, this is not a temporal distinction, and thus it refuses anthropocentrism.

This now requires a formal expressionism that, as Brian Rotman envisions, should push us "outside the domain of the sign." Whereas Meillassoux claims that it is through *mathematics* that his philosophy is able to understand the object in itself (the absolute), the subtitle of Spinoza's *Ethics* (*Ordine Geometrico Demonstrate*) shows that the latter makes use of *geometry* in order to achieve an understanding of the Absolute. Let us map the trajectories sketched.

Mathematics, Geometry, Topology

The relation between mathematics (which includes geometry and topology) and the body is now at stake. Of course Spinoza and Meillassoux are not reductive, nor do they practice a linguisticism. Yet "what mathematics can do" needs more thought.

Contrary to both Spinoza and Meillassoux, there are scholars who do not see how mathematics or a geometrical order would be able to make universal claims. George Lakoff and Rafael E. Núñez (2000, xvi) for instance claim that "[h]uman mathematics, the only kind of mathematics that human beings know, cannot be a subspecies of an abstract transcendental mathematics. Instead, it appears that mathematics as we know it arises from the nature of our brains and our embodied experience." Their book entitled *Where Mathematics Comes From: How the Embodied Mind Brings Mathematics into Being* intends to show that all thought, thus *including* mathematics, follows from our bodily motor existence (which they then presumably consider to be uniquely human). Their arguments are in line with Ricardo Nemirovsky and Francesca Ferrara who claim that "[t]hinking is not a process that takes place 'behind' or 'underneath' bodily activity, but is bodily activity itself" (in Rotman 2008, 33). Claims like these, since they seem to limit mathematics to a bodily interior, are obviously anthropocentric, since all forms of calculus, all formulas and geometrical figures (straight lines, curves, etc.) are then believed to be consequences of our bodily being. By suggesting that mathematical figures necessarily spring from a (human) body, it seems that the figures found outside of us are merely projections of our inside, which then indicates what Meillassoux would call a strong correlationism as it supports "the thesis of the essential inseparability of the act of thinking from its content. All we ever engage with is what is given-to-thought, never an entity subsisting by itself" (Meillassoux [2006] 2008, 36).

Read with Brian Rotman, however, this relation between mathematics and the human body seems to be less confined by the boundary of our skins. In *Becoming Beside Ourselves: The Alphabet, Ghosts, and Distributed Human Being* from 2008 Rotman introduces the concept of "gesture" in order to show how mathematics and the body are one non-linguistic materialist morphogenetic process, countering the general yet largely unacknowledged agreement that in mathematics "Platonism is the contemporary orthodoxy" (Rotman 1997, 18 in Kirby 2003, 422):

> [...] gesture is outside the domain of the sign insofar as signs are coded and call for a hermeneutics, an interpretative apparatus separable from, and in place prior to, the act of signification. Rather, the mode of action of gesture is enactive, exterior to anything prior to its own performance: it works through bodily executed events, creating meaning and mathematical significance 'before one knows it' (2008, 36).

In line with Barad, DeLanda, Massumi, Lloyd, and Meillassoux as well, Rotman calls for mathematics as a key to the ontologically prior. And in contrast with the mathematical anthropocentrism suggested earlier, Rotman does not lock the argument into the body. A gesture always already suggests a kind of rhythm as it necessarily moves *with* the outside object (to come), and *with* the multiplicity in which it happens. Rotman thus proposes that what is at stake concerning a mathematical abstraction is "what it functions with" (Deleuze and Guattari [1980] 1987, 5) thus instead of opposing an abstraction's (or a book's) subject and object, the question is how "[i]t forms a rhizome with the world" (ibid., 11).[2]

Would this necessarily take us "beyond" language? In fact, Kirby in "Enumerating Language: 'The Unreasonable Effectiveness of Mathematics'" from 2003, has a strong argument for approaching mathematics as a language. This does not automatically lead Kirby to a linguisticism and away from the ontological prior. Defining mathematics as a "system of relational configurations that refers to itself," Kirby (2003, 418) alludes to her attempt at rewriting the deflated, representationalist concept of "language" as it features in much of cultural theory, while rewriting "mathematics [as] the language of Nature [...] divine[ly] author[ed]" (ibid., 419) along the way. Kirby thus also critiques Rotman in a manner similar to her and other new materialists' critique of Butler (see Chapter 5 of the present book). Nevertheless, it is possible not to go along with Kirby's negative reading of Rotman's anthropocentrism, based on a simple reversal of a mathematics reated by Nature/God (ibid., 426–427).

It is possible not to go along with Kirby's negative reading of Rotman's anthropocentrism, based on a simple reversal of a mathematics created by Nature/God (ibid., 426–7). That is, we can read the ontological prior into both Kirby and Rotman.

Famously, and counterintuitively via a Derridean detour, Kirby (2006, 84) states that "[f]or if 'there is no outside of text,' as Derrida suggests, then it is in 'the nature of Nature' to write, to read and to model." "[M]atter" thus "appears *within* the horizon of our inquiry as a much more curious subject. And importantly, its appearance need not be veiled in substitute form as a cultural artefact" (ibid., 85; original emphasis). Echoing her rewriting of Ferdinand de Saussure in *Telling Flesh: The Substance of the Corporeal* (1997), Kirby states that Derrida's "there is no outside of text" should be rewritten into "there is no outside of Nature" (Kirby 2008b, 229). Thus, in turn echoing Spinoza, Kirby proclaims a univocity (Colebrook 2004).[3] In this way Rotman's gestural, ontologically prior stance is to be found in Kirby's work when she, via Derrida, states that

> [...] any "unit" is not so much a separate part of a larger whole to which it remains indebted, but rather a unique instantiation of the system's own reinvention (or rewriting) of itself. Thus, every "instance" *is* "the whole," and this imploded, holographic sense of identity confounds linearity as an unfolding sequence of separate, successive moments (Kirby 2003, 425; original emphasis).

We have encountered such theorizations many times in this book, starting with DeLanda's work in the interview with him and in Chapter 5. According to Rotman's "gesture," "the exuberant bodily connectivities" *are* "mathematical practice" (ibid., 428). Kirby's project of showing how "it is [...] in the nature of corporeality to mathematize, represent, or intelligently take measure of itself" (ibid., 434), of "think[ing] of biology as a "unified field" of operational differentiations, a *mathesis naturalis*" (ibid., 438) does exactly the same thing. In both cases, the bodily force is what is ontologically prior.

Then in keeping with how Kirby rewrites the notion of language warding off linguisticism, we should (with Rotman and Deleuze and Guattari, among others) rewrite mathematics warding off a "mathematicism." A necessary breakdown of any mathematical anthropocentrism in favor of any sort of materialism would probably mean, first of all, a move away from set theory, so dominant in mathematics these days (as Fernando Zalamea [forthcoming] also suggests). At least, this is a common move by those scholars interested in what we term a new materialism. Stengers (2000, 157) proposes two routes:

> [...] René Thom pleads for a form of 'nomadic' mathematics, whose vocation would not be to reduce the multiplicity of sensible phenomena to the unity of a mathematical description that would subject them to the order of resemblance, but to construct the mathematical intelligibility of their qualitative difference. The fall of a leaf, then, would no longer be a very complicated case of a Galilean register, but would have to provoke its own mathematics. One could also cite Benoit Mandelbrot's fractal mathematics. Here as well, to 'understand' means to create a language that opens up the possibility of 'encountering' different sensible forms, of reproducing them, without for all that subjugating them to a general law that would give them 'reasons' and allow them to be manipulated.

The first option Stengers proposes is interesting, because of its call to develop a "new materialist" mathematics, focusing on differing (see Chapter 7 of this book), as a worthy alternative to set theory. The second is interesting, because this route is actually the most commonly followed, including by Rotman, DeLanda, and Massumi. Following Mandelbrot's non-Euclidean geometry, it is especially *topology* that is considered as a fruitful ground for a materialist mathematical metaphysics. Topology might even be considered the very opposite of set theory, practicing a radical "difference in degree" as opposed to set-theory's "difference in kind." Bearing this in mind, DeLanda (2002, 24; original emphasis) defines topology as: "[...] the *least differentiated* geometry, the one with the least number of distinct equivalence classes, the one in which many discontinuous forms have blended into one continuous one." Massumi, in his 2002 *Parables for the Virtual: Movement, Affect, Sensation* explains very well how topology should be seen as the smoothest of the sciences, or as Elie Ayache (2010, 147) beautifully puts it: "Mathematics is a thought (and not just a calculus), and it is thought that asserts existence through the orientation of its discourse." Massumi (2002, 135), recalling Kirby, adds to this:

> Topology is not a qualitative science. It is not empirical, if empirical investigation is meant as progressing from description to prediction. It has no predictive value. Incapable of directly referencing anything other than its own variations, it is more analogical than descriptive. It is not, however, an analog *of* anything in particular. It is not an analog in the everyday sense of a variation on a model. Here, there is no model. Only infolding and outfolding: self-referential transformation. The analog is process, self-referenced to its own variations.

Although Meillassoux, in *After Finitude*, seems to be most interested in physics, and sometimes seems to be seduced by set theoretical problems (following the way his teacher Badiou has always been keen on such mathematical models) such as Cantor's theorem, his speculative materialism seems to be in need of a mathematics that actually comes very close to the speculative pragmatism that Massumi has been working on in past years, and notably to the role topology plays in this type of thinking. And vice versa, Meillassoux's interest in the absolute, in searching for the transfinite, or the "unclosed pluralization of the infinite qualities" (Meillassoux [2006] 2008, 142) might be just what Massumi needs when exploring what topology can do. The notion of the virtual (as Massumi takes this from Bergson and Deleuze) especially seems to him of the greatest importance, as affirmed in Meillassoux's "Potentiality and Virtuality" (2011). As Massumi (2002, 135) puts it:

> A topological image center literally makes the virtual appear, in felt thought. It is more apparitional than empirical. Sensation, always on arrival a transformative feeling of the outside, a feeling of thought, is the being of the analog. It is matter in analog mode.

The smoothness of topology is nowadays mostly developed (in maths) in so-called "pointless topology," continuing the traits of Peter T. Johnstone (1977), and mereotopology as it follows Whitehead ([1929/1978] 1985). Here we see most convincingly why Deleuze and Guattari considered mathematics (together with music) capable of producing the smoothest of smooth spaces, and thus as most suitable for a rewriting of the dualisms that haunt us. Johnstone's concept of the "locales" for instance, as he opposes them to "frames," allow us to rethink morphology in terms of "continuous maps" (Johnstone 1982, 39) as he calls them. No longer related to objects, "locales" allow us to do pure morphology that always already includes a multiplicity of bodies *equaling* physical nature. Mathematics (pointless topology) is then our route (among many unforeseen routes) that allows us to get rid of our vectorial (homomorphic) status "in favor of a spreading out on the surface," as Cache (1995, 75) puts it. Our upright position, as the latter continues, would then only be a consequence of the morphologies at work on the continuous abstract map (or plane) that is realized.

To close with an example, we could think of how Massumi (2002, 75) re-reads Michel Serres' analysis of a soccer game, which concludes as follows: "The player's subjectivity is disconnected as he enters the field of potential in and as its sensation. For the play, the player *is* that sensation. The sensation is a channeling of field potential into local action, from which it is again transduced into a global reconfiguration of the field of potential. Sensation is the mode in which potential is present in the perceiving body." The manner in which Massumi does not take man as the starting point of analysis—or even of bodies—but rather the forces and surfaces that are being realized throughout the material practice, opens the way for a pointless topology similar to how Johnstone and contemporary Whiteheadians would have it. Massumi's case proves Johnstone right in introducing a concept like "continuous mapping" when emphasizing the morphogeneses taking place *with* the creation of surfaces. Freeing us from the point, the line and even from movement (which in the end makes up a correlationist argument, as Meillassoux would put it), the virtual absolute is actualized. Pointless topology is then one of the "infinity mechanisms" in which Henri Michaux ([1972] 2002, 70) finds himself: the one infinite mechanism that is all. It liberates a new materialism.

Notes

1. Here it should be mentioned once again that French feminist theories, in contradistinction to the works reviewed and synthesized by Harding, have dealt with Lloyd's monist question, and that this minor tradition in feminist theory has been our main source of inspiration. When Braidotti (2011a) writes that "Colebrook (2000a) suggests that a younger feminist wave is looking at the question of sexual difference as not only or primarily a question that concerns the subject or the subject's body," she is referring precisely to the way in which a monism actually shifts anthropocentrism. Colebrook provocatively calls this new feminist materialism "a materialism without bodies." Colebrook used this term at the conference "What is the Matter with Materialism?," Utrecht University, October 25, 2010.

2. Rather than implicitly accepting a humanism or anthropocentrism, Rotman (and Deleuze and Guattari)'s mathematics of gesture seem(s) to engage with what Stengers has called a "cosmopolitical network" or what Latour refers to as "the Parliament of Things" (see also Lischka 2007: 40). In line with Rotman, Latour ([1991] 1993: 142) considers the sciences to be of interest (to politics) because of its intensities that are both human and non-human, both material and immaterial, indeed, that flow contingently:

   > [...] we continue to believe in the sciences, but instead of taking in their objectivity, their truth, their coldness, their extraterritoriality—qualities they never had, except after the arbitrary withdrawal of epistemology—we retain what has always been most interesting about them: their daring, their experimentation, their uncertainty, their warmth, their incongruous blend of hybrids, their crazy ability to reconstitute the social bond.

3. This goes beyond the claim found in *Telling Flesh*, which reads: "[...] we think of the referent as neither preceding nor following language because it is an immanence within it" (Kirby 1997: 19). Where the earlier Kirby seems to prioritise language—the referent being an immanence within language—the later Kirby comes to evoke a univocity that comes close to Deleuze and Guattari when they state in *A Thousand Plateaus*: "There are variables of expression *that establish a relation between language and the outside, but precisely because they are immanent to language*" (Deleuze and Guattari [1980] 1987: 82; original emphasis). Here, we do not look at language, but at immediate circumstantial expression and implied collective assemblages. Mathematics' "reference to itself" should be read in the latter manner.

Bibliography

Ahmed, S. 2008. "Open Forum Imaginary Prohibitions: Some Preliminary Remarks on the Founding Gestures of the 'New Materialism.'" *European Journal of Women's Studies* 15(1): 23–39.

Alaimo, S and S. Hekman, eds. 2008. *Material Feminisms*. Bloomington and Indianapolis: Indiana University Press.

Alcoff, L. 2000. "Philosophy Matters: A Review of Recent Work in Feminist Philosophy." *Signs: Journal of Women in Culture and Society* 25(3): 841–82.

Artaud, A. 1971. "Notes sur les Cultures Orientales." *Oeuvres Completes*, Tome VIII. Paris: Gallimard.

Ayache, E. 2010. *The Blank Swan: The End of Probability*. Melbourne: re.press.

Badiou, A. 1999. *Deleuze: The Clamor of Being*. Translated by L. Burchill. Minneapolis and London: University of Minnesota Press.

---. 2007. *The Concept of Model: An Introduction to the Materialist Epistemology of Mathematics*. Translated by Z. L. Fraser. Melbourne: re.press.

Balibar, É. [1989] 1998. "Politics and Communication," in *Spinoza and Politics*. London and New York: Verso, 99–124.

Barad, K. 2001. "Re(con)figuring Space, Time, and Matter," in *Feminist Locations: Global and Local, Theory and Practice*. Edited by M. DeKoven. New Brunswick: Rutgers University Press, 75–109.

---. 2003. "Posthumanist Performativity: Toward an Understanding of How Matter Comes to Matter." *Signs: Journal of Women in Culture and Society* 28(3): 801–31.

---. 2007. *Meeting the Universe Halfway: Quantum Physics and the Entanglement of Matter and Meaning*. Durham and London: Duke University Press.

---. 2010. "Quantum Entanglements and Hauntological Relations of Inheritance: Dis/continuities, SpaceTime Enfoldings, and Justice-to-Come." *Derrida Today* 3(2): 240–68.

Baudrillard, J. [1981] 1995. *Simulacra and Simulation*. Translated by S. F. Glaser. Ann Arbor: University of Michigan Press.

---. [1995] 1996. *The Perfect Crime*. Translated by Ch. Turner. London and New York: Verso.

Benjamin, W. [1982] 2002. *The Arcades Project*. Translated by H. Eiland and K. McLaughlin. Cambridge and London: Belknap/Harvard University Press.

Bergson, H. [1896] 2004. *Matter and Memory*. 5th ed., translated by N. M. Paul and W. Scott Palmer. Mineola, NY: Dover.

---. [1907] 1998. *Creative Evolution*. Translated by A. Mitchell. Mineola, NY: Dover Publications.

---. [1934] 2007. *The Creative Mind: An Introduction to Metaphysics*. Translated by M. L. Andison. Mineola, NY: Dover Publications.

Bleeker, M. 2008. "Passages in Post-Modern Theory: Mapping the Apparatus." *Parallax* 14(1): 55–67.

Bolt, B. and E. Barrett eds. Forthcoming. *Carnal Knowledge: Towards a New Materialism Through the Arts*. London: IBTauris.

Braidotti, R. 1991. *Patterns of Dissonance: A Study of Women and Contemporary Philosophy*. Cambridge: Polity Press.

---. 1994. *Nomadic Subjects: Embodiment and Sexual Difference in Contemporary Feminist Theory*. New York: Columbia University Press.

---. 2000. "Teratologies," in *Deleuze and Feminist Theory*, edited by I. Buchanan and C. Colebrook, 156–72. Edinburgh: Edinburgh University Press.

---. 2002a. *Metamorphoses: Towards a Materialist Theory of Becoming.* Cambridge: Polity Press.

---. 2002b. "Identity, Subjectivity, Difference: A Critical Genealogy," in *Thinking Differently: A Reader in European Women's Studies*, edited by G. Griffin and R. Braidotti, 158–80. London and New York: Zed Books.

---. 2006. *Transpositions: On Nomadic Ethics.* Cambridge: Polity Press.

---. 2008. "In Spite of the Times: The Postsecular Turn in Feminism." *Theory, Culture and Society* 25(6): 1–24.

---. 2011a. *Nomadic Theory: The Portable Rosi Braidotti.* New York: Columbia University Press.

---. 2011b. *Nomadic Subjects: Embodiment and Sexual Difference in Contemporary Feminist Theory.* Second edition. New York: Columbia University Press

---. ed. 2010. *The History of Continental Philosophy.* Vol. 7. Durham: Acumen.

Bryant, L., N. Srnicek and G. Harman eds. 2011. *The Speculative Turn: Continental Materialism and Realism.* Melbourne: re.press.

Butler, J. 1986. "Sex and Gender in Simone de Beauvoir's Second Sex." *Yale French Studies* 72: 35–49.

---. [1987] 1999. *Subjects of Desire: Hegelian Reflections in Twentieth Century France.* New York: Columbia University Press.

---. 1993. *Bodies that Matter: On the Discursive Limits of 'Sex.'* New York and London: Routledge.

---. 2009. *Frames of War: When is Life Grievable?* London and New York: Verso.

Butler, J. and J. W. Scott eds. 1992. *Feminists Theorize the Political.* New York: Routledge.

Cache, B. 1995. *Earth Moves, the Furnishing of Territories.* Edited by M. Speaks Translated by A. Boyman. Cambridge and London: The MIT Press.

Changfoot, N. 2009a. "*The Second Sex*'s Continued Relevance for Equality and Difference Feminisms." *European Journal of Women's Studies* 16(1): 11–31.

---. 2009b. "Transcendence in Simone De Beauvoir's *The Second Sex*: Revisiting Masculinist Ontology." *Philosophy and Social Criticism* 35(4): 391–410.

Cheah, P. 1996. "Mattering." *Diacritics* 26(1): 108–39.

Cixous, H. [1975] 1976. "The Laugh of the Medusa." Translated by K. Cohen & P. Cohen. *Signs: Journal of Women in Culture and Society*, 1(4): 875–93.

Colebrook, C. 2002. *Understanding Deleuze*. Sydney: Allen and Unwin.

---. 2004. "Postmodernism is a Humanism: Deleuze and Equivocity." *Women: A Cultural Review* 15(3): 283–307.

---. 2008. "On Not Becoming Man: The Materialist Politics of Unactualized Potential," in *Material Feminisms*. Edited by S. Alaimo and S. Hekman, 52–84. Bloomington and Indianapolis: Indiana University Press.

Connolly, W. 1999. *Why am I not a secularist?* Minneapolis: University of Minnesota Press.

Coole, D. and S. Frost, eds. (2010). *New Materialisms: Ontology, Agency, and Politics*. Durham and London: Duke University Press.

Culler, J. [1982] 2008. *On Deconstruction: Theory and Criticism after Structuralism*. 25th Anniversary Edition. London and New York: Routledge.

Davis, N. 2009. "New Materialism and Feminism's Anti-Biologism: A Response to Sara Ahmed." *European Journal of Women's Studies* 16(1): 67–80.

de Beauvoir, S. [1949] 2010. *The Second Sex*. Translated by C. Borde and S. Malovany-Chevallier. New York: Alfred A. Knopf.

de Beistegui, M. 2004. *Truth and Genesis: Philosophy as Differential Ontology*. Bloomington: Indiana University Press.

De Boever, A, A. Murray, and J. Roffe. 2009. "'Technical Mentality' Revisited: Brian Massumi on Gilbert Simondon." *Parrhesia: A Journal of Critical Philosophy* 7: 36–45.

DeLanda, M. 1996. "The Geology of Morals: A Neo-Materialist Interpretation." http://www.t0.or.at/delanda/geology.htm (accessed June 12, 2009).

---. 1997. *A Thousand Years of Nonlinear History*. New York: Zone Books.

---. 2002. *Intensive Science & Virtual Philosophy*. London and New York: Continuum.

---. 2006. *A New Philosophy of Society: Assemblage Theory and Social Complexity*. London and New York: Continuum.

Deleuze, G. [1956/2002] 2004. "Bergson's Conception of Difference," in *Desert Islands and Other Texts 1953–1974*, edited by D. Lapoujade, 32–51. Translated by M. Taormina. Semiotext(e) Foreign Agents Series. Cambridge and London: The MIT Press.

---. [1966] 1991. *Bergsonism*. Translated by H. Tomlinson and B. Habberjam. New York: Zone Books.

---. [1968] 1994. *Difference and Repetition*. Translated by P. Patton. New York: Columbia University Press.

---. [1969] 1990. *The Logic of Sense*. Edited by C. V. Boundas. Translated by M. Lester and Ch. Stivale. New York: Columbia University Press.

---. [1981] 1988. *Spinoza, Practical Philosophy*. Translated by R. Hurley. San Francisco: City Lights.

---. [1985] 2000. *Cinema 2: The Time-Image*. Translated by H. Tomlinson and R. Galeta. Minneapolis: University of Minnesota Press.

---. [1988] 1995. "On Philosophy," in *Negotiations 1972–1990*, 135–55. Translated by M. Joughin. New York: Columbia University Press.

---. 1997. "Desire and Pleasure," in *Foucault and his Interlocutors*, edited by A. I. Davidson, 183–92. Chicago and London: University of Chicago Press.

---. 2006. *Two Regimes of Madness: Texts and Interviews 1975–1995*. Edited by D. Lapoujade. Translated by A. Hodges and M. Taormina. New York: Semiotext(e).

Deleuze, G. and F. Guattari. [1972] 1983. *Anti-Oedipus: Capitalism and Schizophrenia*. Translated by R. Hurley, M. Seem and H. R. Lane. Minneapolis: University of Minnesota Press.

---. [1980] 1987. *A Thousand Plateaus: Capitalism and Schizophrenia*. Translated by B. Massumi. Minneapolis: University of Minnesota Press.

---. [1991] 1994. *What is Philosophy?* Translated by H. Tomlinson and G. Burchell. New York: Columbia University Press.

Derrida, J. [1968] 1982. Différance. *Margins of Philosophy*. Translated by A. Bass. Chicago: The University of Chicago Press.

---. [1985] 1988. "Letter to a Japanese Friend," in *Derrida and Difference*, edited by D. Wood and R. Bernasconi, 270–76. Evanston: Northwestern University Press.

---. [1993] 2006. *Specters of Marx: The State of the Debt, the Work of Mourning and the New International*. Translated by P. Kamuf. New York and London: Routledge.

Dolphijn, R. 2004. *Foodscapes: Towards a Deleuzian Ethics of Consumption*. Delft: Eburon.

---. 2010. "Cultural Studies," in *The Sage Encyclopedia of Identity, Vol. 2*, edited by R. L. Jackson, 173–80. London: Sage.

---. 2011. "'Man is Ill Because He is Badly Constructed': Artaud, Klossowski and Deleuze in Search for the Earth Inside." *Deleuze Studies* 5(1): 18–34

Foucault, M. [1966/1970] 1994. *The Order of Things: An Archaeology of the Human Sciences*. New York: Vintage.

---. [1970] 1998. "Theatrum Philosophicum," in *Essential Works of Foucault, 1954–1984, Vol 2: Aesthetics, Method, and Epistemology*, edited by J. D. Faubion, M. Foucault and P. Rabinow, 343–68. New York: New Press.

---. 1980. *Power-Knowledge: Selected Interviews and Other Writings, 1972–1977*. Brighton: Harvester Press.

---. 2008. *Introduction to Kant's Anthropology*. Edited by R. Nigro. Translated by R. Nogro and K. Briggs. Los Angeles: Semiotext(e).

---. 2003. *"Society Must Be Defended": Lectures at the College De France, 1975–76*. Edited by M. Bertani and A. Fontana. Translated by D. Macey. New York: Picador.

Fraser, M. 2002. "What is the Matter of Feminist Criticism?" *Economy and Society* 31(4): 606–25.

Fukuyama, F. 2002. *Our Posthuman Future: Consequences of the BioTechnological Revolution*. London: Profile Books.

Gallagher, S. 2005. *How the Body Shapes the Mind*. Oxford: Clarendon Press.

Gatens, M. 2003. "Beauvoir and Biology: A Second Look," in *The Cambridge Companion to Simone de Beauvoir*, edited by C. Card. 266–85. Cambridge: Cambridge University Press.

Gatens, M. and G. Lloyd. 1999. *Collective Imaginings: Spinoza, Past and Present*. London and New York: Routledge.

Genosko, G. 1996. *The Guattari Reader*. Oxford and Cambridge: Blackwell.

Grosz, E. [1993] 1994. "A Thousand Tiny Sexes: Feminism and Rhizomatics." In *Gilles Deleuze and the Theatre of Philosophy*, edited by C.V. Boundas and D. Olkowski, 187–210. London and New York: Routledge.

---. 1994. *Volatile Bodies: Toward a Corporeal Feminism*. Sydney: Allen and Unwin.

---. 2000. "Histories of a Feminist Future." *Signs: Journal of Women in Culture and Society* 25(4): 1017–21.

---. 2005. *Time Travels: Feminism, Nature, Power*. Durham and London: Duke University Press.

Guattari, F. [1964] 1984. *Transversality. Molecular Revolution: Psychiatry and Politics*. Translated by R. Sheed. Harmondsworth: Penguin Books.

Guattari, F. and S. Rolnik. [1982] 2008. "Emotion, Energy, Body, Sex," in *Molecular Revolution in Brazil*. Translated by K. Clapshow and B. Holmes. Los Angeles, *Semiotext(e)*: 403–12.

Habermas, J. 2003. *The Future of Human Nature*. Cambridge: Polity Press.

Halewood, M. 2009. "Language, Subjectivity and Individuality," in *Deleuze, Whitehead, Bergson: Rhizomatic Connections*, edited by K. Robinson. London: Palgrave Macmillan, 45–60.

Hames-García, M. 2008. "How Real is Race?," in *Material Feminisms*, edited by S. Alaimo and S. Hekman, 308–39. Bloomington: Indiana University Press.

Hansell, M. (2007). *Built by Animals: The Natural History of Animal Architecture*. Oxford and New York: Oxford University Press.

Haraway, D. 1988. "Situated Knowledges: *The Science Question in Feminism* and the Privilege of Partial Perspective." *Feminist Studies* 14(3): 575–99.

---. 1997. *Modest_Witness@Second_Millennium. FemaleMan©_Meets_OncoMouse™*. London and New York: Routledge.

---. 2003. *The Companion Species Manifesto: Dogs, People, and Significant Otherness*. Chicago: Prickly Paradigm Press.

---. 2008. *When Species Meet*. Minneapolis: The University of Minnesota Press.

Harding, S. 1986. *The Science Question in Feminism*. Milton Keynes: Open University Press.

---. 1991. *Whose Science? Whose Knowledge?* Milton Keynes: Open University Press.

Harding, S. and U. Narayan. 2000. *Decentering the Center: Philosophy for a Multicultural, Postcolonial, and Feminist World*. Bloomington: Indiana University Press.

Harman, G. 2008. "DeLanda's Ontology: Assemblage and Realism." *Continental Philosophy Review* 41 (3): 367–83.

---. 2010. "Objects, Matter, Sleep, and Death," in *Towards Speculative Realism: Essays and Lectures*. Winchester, UK: Zero Books.

---. 2011a. "On the Undermining of Objects: Grant, Bruno, and Radical Philosophy," in *The Speculative Turn: Continental Materialism and Realism*, edited by L. Bryant, N. Srnicek, and G. Harman. Melbourne: re.press, 21–40.

---. 2011b. *Quentin Meillassoux: Philosophy in the Making*. Edinburgh: Edinburgh University Press.

Harris, G. J. 2003. "Afterword: Walk Like an Egyptian," in *Performing Transversally: Reimagining Shakespeare and the Critical Future*. Edited by B. Reynolds. New York and Baskingstoke: Palgrave Macmillan, 271–86.

Hartsock, N. 1987. "Re-thinking Modernism: Minority vs. Majority Theories." *Cultural Critique* 7: 187–206.

Hegel, G.W.F. [1807] 1977. *Phenomenology of Spirit*. Translated by A.V. Miller. Oxford: Oxford University Press.

Heidegger, M. [1959] 1971. "A Dialogue on Language between a Japanese and an Inquirer," in *On the Way to Language*, 1–56. Translated by P.D. Hertz. New York: Harper & Row.

---. 1954. "Die Frage nach Technik," in *Vorträge und Aufsätze*. Pfullingen: Verlag Günther Neske.

---. 1960. *Der Ursprung des Kunstwerkes*. Stuttgart: Reclam.

---. [1980] 1994. *Hegel's Phenomenology of Spirit*. Translated by P. Emad and K. Maly. Bloomington and Indianapolis: Indiana University Press.

Heinämaa, S. 1997. "What is a Woman? Butler and Beauvoir on the Foundations of the Sexual Difference." *Hypatia: A Journal of Feminist Philosophy* 12(1): 20–39.

Hekman, S. 2010. *The Material of Knowledge: Feminist Disclosures*. Bloomington and Indianapolis: Indiana University Press.

Hill, R. 2008. "Phallocentrism in Bergson: Life and Matter." *Deleuze Studies* 2 (supplement *Deleuze and Gender*. Edited by C. Colebrook and J. Weinstein): 123–36.

Hird, M.J. 2004. "Feminist Matters: New Materialist Considerations of Sexual Difference." *Feminist Theory* (5)2: 223–32.

---. 2006. "Animal Transex." *Australian Feminist Studies* 21(49): 35–50.

Holland, E. 1999. *Deleuze and Guattari's Anti-Oedipus: Introduction to Schizoanalysis*. London and New York: Routledge.

Hughes, A. and Witz, A. 1997. "Feminism and the Matter of Bodies: From de Beauvoir to Butler." *Body & Society* 3(1): 47–60.

Johnstone, P.T. 1977. *Topos Theory*. London, New York and San Francisco: Academic Press.

---. 1982. *Stone Spaces*. Cambridge, New York and Victoria: The Press Syndicate of the University of Cambridge.

Kant, I. [1781, 1787] 1998. *Critique of Pure Reason*. Second edition. Translated by P. Guyer and A. W. Wood. Cambridge: Cambridge University Press.

---. [1790] 2000. *Critique of Judgment*. Translated by P. Guyer and E. Matthews. Cambridge: Cambridge University Press.

---. [1788] 1996. *Critique of Practical Reason*. Translated and edited by M. J. Gregor. *Practical Philosophy*. M. J. Gregor. Cambridge: Cambridge University Press, 139–271.

---. [1800] 1988. *Logic*. New York, Dover Publications.

---. 2005. *Notes and Fragments*. Translated by P. Guyer, C. Bowman and F. Rauscher. Cambridge: Cambridge University Press.

Kelly, J. 1979. "The Doubled Vision of Feminist Theory: A Postscript to the 'Women and Power' Conference." *Feminist Studies* 5(1): 216–27.

Kirby, V. 1997. *Telling Flesh: The Substance of the Corporeal*. New York and London: Routledge.

---. 2003. "Enumerating Language: 'The Unreasonable Effectiveness of Mathematics'." *Configurations* 11(3): 417–39.

---. 2006. *Judith Butler: Live Theory*. London and New York: Continuum.

---. 2008a. "Subject to Natural Law: A Meditation on the 'Two Cultures' Problem." *Australian Feminist Studies* 23(55): 5–17.

---. 2008b. "Natural Convers(at)ions: or, what if Culture was really Nature all along?," in *Material Feminisms*, edited by S. Alaimo and S. Hekman. Bloomington: Indiana University Press, 214–36

---. 2010. "Original Science: Nature Deconstructing Itself." *Derrida Today* 3.2: 201–20.

---. 2011. *Quantum Anthropologies: Life at Large*. Durham and London: Duke University Press.

Kochhar-Lindgren, G. 2011. *Philosophy, Art and the Specters of Marx*. Amherst, New York: Cambria Press.

Kruks, S. 2005. "Beauvoir's Time/ Our Time: The Renaissance in Simone de Beauvoir Studies." *Feminist Studies* 31(2): 286–309.

Lakoff, G. and R.E. Núñez. 2000. *Where Mathematics Comes From: How the Embodied Mind Brings Mathematics into Being*. New York: Basic Books.

Latour, B. [1991] 1993. *We Have Never Been Modern*. Translated by C. Porter. London: Prentice Hall.

---. 2004. "Why Has Critique Run Out of Steam? From Matters of Fact to Matters of Concern." *Critical Inquiry* 30: 225–48.

Lauretis, T. de. 1986. *Feminist Studies, Critical Studies*. Bloomington: Indiana University Press.

---. 1994. *The Practice of Love: Lesbian Sexuality and Perverse Desire*. Bloomington: Indiana University Press.

Leibniz, G. [1714] 1962. "The Monadology," in *Discourse on Metaphysics, Correspondence with Arnauld and Monadology*, 251–72. Translated by G. R. Montgomery. La Salle, IL: The Open Court Publishing House.

Lingis, A. 1994. *The Community of Those who have Nothing In Common*. Bloomington: Indiana University Press.

Lischka, C. 2007. "Mechano Poïia," in *Mechanics as Agency: Artistic Perspectives*, edited by C. Lischka and A. Sick, 36–47. Bielefeld: Transscript Verlag.

Lloyd, G. [1984] 1993. *The Man of Reason: 'Male' and 'Female' in Western Philosophy*. New York: Routledge.

Lyon, J. 1999. *Manifestoes: Provocations of the Modern*. Ithaca and London: Cornell University Press.

Lyotard, J-F. [1988] 1991. *The Inhuman: Reflections on Time*. Translated by G. Bennington and R. Bowlby. Stanford, CA: Stanford University Press.

Mahmood, S. 2005. *Politics of Piety: The Islamic Revival and the Feminist Subject*. Princeton: Princeton University Press.

Massumi, B. 2002. *Parables for the Virtual: Movement, Affect, Sensation*. Durham and London: Duke University Press.

Meillassoux, Q. [2006] 2008. *After Finitude: An Essay on the Necessity of Contingency*. Translated by R. Brassier. New York: Continuum.

---. 2010. "Que peut dire la métaphysique sur ces temps de crise?" *L'Annuel des Idees* February 5, 2010. http://www.annuel-idees.fr/2-Que-peut-dire-la-metaphysique.html (accessed June 1, 2011).

---. 2011. "Potentiality and Virtuality," translated by R. Mackay, in *The Speculative Turn: Continental Materialism and Realism*, edited by L. Bryant, N. Srnicek, and G. Harman, Melbourne: re.press, 224–36.

Michaux, H. [1972] 2002. *Miserable Miracle*. New York: New York Review Books.

Mol, A. 2002. *The Body Multiple: Ontology in Medical Practice*. Durham and London: Duke University Press.

Mullarkey, J. 2006. *Post-Continental Philosophy: An Outline*. London and New York: Continuum.

Nelson, L. H. 1993. "Epistemological Communities," in *Feminist Epistemologies*, edited by L. Alcoff and E. Potter. New York: Routledge, 121–59.

Nietzsche, F.W. [1883–1885] 1967. *Also Sprach Zarathustra*. Edited by G. Colli and M. Montinari. Berlin: Walter de Gruyter & Co.

Rahman, M. and A. Witz. 2003. "What Really Matters? The Elusive Quality of the Material in Feminist Thought." *Feminist Theory* 4(3): 243–61.

Rich, A. 1976. *Of Woman Born: Motherhood as Experience and Institution*. New York: Norton.

---. 1985. *Blood, Bread and Poetry: Selected Prose, 1979–1985*. New York: Norton.

Rossini, M. 2006. "To the Dogs: Companion Speciesism and the New Feminist Materialism." *Kritikos: An International and Interdisciplinary Journal of Postmodern Cultural Sound, Text and Image* 3. http://intertheory.org/rossini Last accessed: April 8, 2008.

Rotman, B. 2008. *Becoming Beside Ourselves: The Alphabet, Ghosts, and Distributed Human Being*. Durham and London: Duke University Press.

Saldanha, A. 2006. "Reontologising Race: The Machinic Geography of Phenotype." *Environment and Planning D: Society and Space* 24(1): 9–24.

Schrader, A. (2010). "Responding to *Pfiesteria piscicida* (the Fish Killer): Phantomatic Ontologies, Indeterminacy, and Responsibility in Toxic Microbiology." *Social Studies of Science* 40(2): 275–306.

Scott, J. W. 1996. *Only Paradoxes to Offer: French Feminists and the Rights of Man*. Cambridge and London: Harvard University Press.

---. 2007. *The Politics of the Veil*. Princeton: Princeton University Press.

Serres, M. with B. Latour. 1995. "Third Conversation: Demonstration and Interpretation," in *Conversations on Science, Culture, and Time*, 77–123. Ann Arbor: The University of Michigan Press.

Shaviro, S. 2009. *Without Criteria; Kant, Whitehead, Deleuze and Aesthetics*. Cambridge, Mass. and London: The MIT Press.

Sheridan, S. 2002. "Words and Things: Some Feminist Debates on Culture and Materialism." *Australian Feminist Studies* 17(37): 23–30.

Simondon, G. [1958] 1980. *On the Mode of Existence of Technical Objects*. Translated by N. Mellamphy. University of Western Ontario. http://dephasage.ocular-witness.com/pdf/SimondonGilbert.OnTheModeOfExistence.pdf (accessed March 13, 2011).

---. 2009. "The Position of the Problem of Ontogenesis." Translated by G. Flanders. *Parrhesia* 7: 4–16.

Snow, C.P. [1959] 1965. *The Two Cultures: and A Second Look*. London: Cambridge University Press.

Sönser Breen, M. and W.J. Blumenfeld eds. 2005. *Butler Matters: Judith Butler's Impact on Feminist and Queer Studies*. Hampshire and Burlington: Ashgate.

Spinoza [1677] 2001. *Ethics*. Translated by W.H. White. Revised by A. H. Stirling. With an Introduction by Don Garrett. Ware: Hertfordshire.

Squier, S. and M. M. Littlefield. 2004. Feminist Theory and/of Science: Feminist Theory Special Issue. *Feminist Theory* 5(2): 123–6.

Stengers, I. 2000. *The Invention of Modern Science*. Minneapolis: Minnesota University Press.

Thornham, S. 2000. *Feminist Theory and Cultural Studies: Stories of Unsettled Relations*. London: Arnold.

Tiedemann, R. 2005. "Historical Materialism or Political Messianism? An interpretation of the thesis "On the Concept of History," in *Walter Benjamin: Critical Evaluations in Cultural Theory*, edited by P. Osborne. New York: Routledge, 137–69.

Turing, A.M. 1950. "Computing Machinery and Intelligence." *Mind* 59: 433–60.

van der Tuin, I. 2008. "Deflationary Logic: Response to Sara Ahmed's 'Imaginary Prohibitions: Some Preliminary Remarks on the Founding Gestures of the 'New Materialism.'" *European Journal of Women's Studies* 15(4): 411–6.

---. 2009. "'Jumping Generations:' On Second- and Third-Wave Feminist Epistemology." *Australian Feminist Studies* (special issue: *Generation: On Feminist Time-Lines*. C. Colebrook and R. Braidotti) 24(59): 17–31.

---. 2011. "'A Different Starting Point, a Different Metaphysics': Reading Bergson and Barad Diffractively." *Hypatia: A Journal of Feminist Philosophy* 26(1): 22–42.

Vintges, K. [1992] 1996. *Philosophy as Passion: The Thinking of Simone de Beauvoir*. Translated by A. Lavelle. Bloomington and Indianapolis: Indiana University Press.

Ware, V. 1992. *Beyond the Pale: White Women, Racism and History*. London and New York: Verso.

Welchman, A. 2005. "Materialism," in *The Edinburgh Dictionary of Continental Philosophy*, edited by J. Protevi, 388–91. Edinburgh: Edinburgh University Press.

Whitehead, A.N. [1925] 1997. *Science and the Modern World*. New York: Free Press.

---. [1929/1978] 1985. *Process and Reality*. New York: Free Press.

Wiegman, R. 2002. *Women's Studies On Its Own: A Next Wave Reader in Institutional Change*. Durham: Duke University Press.

Wilbert, C. 2006. "Profit, Plague and Poultry: The Intra-active Worlds of Highly Pathogenic Avian Flu." *Radical Philosophy* (September/ October 2006). http://www.radicalphilosophy.com/default.asp?channel_id=2187&editorial_id=22192 (accessed June 11, 2009).

Zalamea, F. Forthcoming. *Synthetic Philosophy of Contemporary Mathematics. Urbanomic.* Translated by Z. L. Fraser. London: Urbanomic.

Permissions

Chapter 5 is reprinted with the kind permission of Taylor & Francis Ltd., and originally appeared as "The Transversality of New Materialism," by Iris van der Tuin and Rick Dolphijn, *Women: A Cultural Review* 21.2 (2010): 153–71.

Chapter 6 is reprinted with the equally kind permission of Springer Science+Business Media, and originally appeared as "On the philosophical impetus of a new materialism," by Rick Dolphijn and Iris van der Tuin, *Continental Philosophy* Review, 44, 2011, 383–400.

Printed in Great Britain
by Amazon